And Forgive Us Our Debts

And Forgive Us Our Debts

By
Gerald Gould
With Debra Ciskey

25th Anniversary Edition

Edited by
B.B. Gould

Hawk & Hummingbird Press
Miami, Florida
Copyright © 2014 by B.B. Gould

All rights reserved.
No part of this book may be reproduced by any mechanical, photographic,
or electronic process, nor may it be stored in a retrieval system, transmitted,
or otherwise be copied for public or private use.

First Edition, 1989
Published in Miami, Florida

Revised 25th Anniversary Edition, 2014

Dedication

For the professional debt collectors in the more than 3,000 member offices of the American Collectors Association, Inc. (ACA), the ACA staff in Minneapolis, MN, and most especially for my wife, Johnalene, who has always been my constant, albeit reluctant, partner in our business adventure.

"If man loves the labor of his trade,
Apart from any question of success or fame
The gods have called him"
Robert Louis Stevenson

Acknowledgments

To anyone who has ever had the desire to lift up the writings and thoughts of others, you know the joys and struggles of penning a heartfelt dedication. Were it not for my dear husband, Gerry, I would never have known about all of the ins and outs of a professional debt collector. When I decided to take his typewritten copy and digitize it, I had no idea it would be so much fun. From the beginning, I realized someone should read through it for typos and an extra set of eyes. That someone was Vi Lorenc, a dear angel who encouraged me from the start.

Along the way I enlisted my good friend and fellow author, Kathleen J. Callanan. Her insight and understanding kept me going. Because of her encouragement I was able to "rev my engines and get it done."

Cary Bayer, my life coach of many years, believed in me and provided the spirit and environment for this project. I am grateful for his introduction to designer, Jeff Williamson. Jeff has been a master at creating just the right look. Thanks to all of these friends and mentors.

Finally I would like to thank Kevin Gaffer, CEO of Renkim Co. for sponsoring the production of this 25th Anniversary edition of *And Forgive Us Our Debts*. Debra Ciskey suggested that I approach Kevin with the idea of distributing this book to all attendees at the 75th annual convention of ACA International. As one of the largest vendors to the industry, Kevin and the Renkim Co. made this edition possible.

Table of Contents

Forward to the 25th Anniversary Edition 9
Prologue 11
About the Sketches 13

Chapter 1	Answered…One Lingering Question	15
Chapter 2	To Be or Not to Be…Self-employed in the Collection Business	25
Chapter 3	The Best Feeling on Earth?	31
Chapter 4	Some Things My Grandparents Never Told Me That I'm Telling You	35
Chapter 5	Collecting Can Be Hazardous to Your Health	47
Chapter 6	Images, Stereotypes, Heroes and Heroines	53
Chapter 7	Bodies and Souls	61
Chapter 8	"The Check is in the Mail"	69
Chapter 9	Those that Can, Do…And also Teach	79
Chapter 10	Please Call Me Coach	91
Chapter 11	Debtors' Letters	101
Chapter 12	Time Flies When You're Having Fun	115
Chapter 13	Collections from Cave Man to the Computer	125
Chapter 14	I Had the Craziest Dream	135
Chapter 15	Having the Last Word	143

About the Authors 145

2014 Forward

I met Gerry Gould when I was Director of Education at the Association for Credit and Collection Professionals (now known as ACA International, the association of credit and collection professionals.) I fell in love with Gerry immediately—oh, not the "until death do us part" kind of love—but the kind of love you feel for someone who is clearly passionate about life and his role in the world. I met Gerry in Miami, where he lived, and where ACA held annual "Collection Business Academy" meetings for several years starting about 1986. Gerry was a certified instructor for ACA, and I was responsible for corralling our faculty, providing them training and support, and working with them to keep our schools, as they were called at the time, up to date. There was one school in particular that Gerry loved—the Skiptracing School. Skiptracing, the art of finding people who don't want to be found, was a particular interest of Gerry's and he had about a million stories he could tell about finding people who had tried to evade their creditors and debt collectors. Gerry had an entertaining way of telling a story and teaching that enamored him to his students. Because the Skiptracing school badly needed updating, Gerry and I worked together to incorporate new techniques and sources for information that he successfully used. This was before the automated, batch skiptracing we all use today was widely available—Gerry wanted to teach people how to find that one person, one at a time. He sent me material which I edited, and we got an updated school launched.

Working on that seminar with me was the catalyst Gerry needed to tell me about the book he was writing, and his vision for the finished product. He asked me if I would consider editing his book so he could self-publish it. The timing was right—I was about to take a leave of absence for about 6 weeks because I was close to delivering my second baby. I agreed and off we went. It took some time longer than the anticipated 6 weeks to get it all done, and Gerry worked with his illustrators and it finally got done.

As ACA International celebrates its 75th anniversary, it is my pleasure to see *And Forgive Us our Debts* in distribution. I hope you enjoy Gerry's stories, and best wishes for prosperity and success!

Debra Ciskey, *Editor*
2014

Prologue

Some people enjoy being the first to try something new. Then there are others who never try anything new. I've never considered myself to be a pioneer. If I had been a contemporary of Christopher Columbus I would not have been a member of his crew on that first expedition. You would not have seen me in the first caravan as our infant nation headed west. And now that we are in the midst of the space age my name does not appear with those waiting to be the first passengers to the moon.

And yet in July, 1950, I found myself moving to a relatively young city and about to enter an infant industry long before there were state and federal laws governing that industry, long before there was an effective education program to train agency personnel and long before we were involved with computerized offices and cardless systems. Perhaps I was a pioneer after all.

I've lost count of the number of times during the past 37 years that I've promised myself to write a book about my experiences operating a small collection agency. But then there were the distractions: the pressures of the daily routine, raising a family, more important priorities and the lingering doubt that I could not see it through. But no matter how long or wide the detour I always returned to telling myself, "You have a book to write." There came a time when I eventually asked myself whether or not I was really serious or just whistling in the wind.

One of the techniques I have used through the years to put an end to my procrastination is to tell someone about the plan. Early in 1986, Debra Ciskey, Director of Education for the Association for Credit and Collection Professionals, ACA, asked me to help in the revision of the ACA Skiptracing School. I was so impressed with what she did with the information I provided her that when we were finished I asked her if she would like to collaborate with me in writing the book. I was even a bit surprised when she said yes. She was about to begin a maternity leave and thought that would be the best time to help me. For this I will remain forever grateful to Debra. I'm convinced that had she said no I would still be looking at myself in the mirror periodically saying "You've got to get started…" instead of sitting at the typewriter.

I have never found it unprofitable to stop from time to time in my life and look back and reflect on where I have been, where I am now and where I am going. It's an exercise I highly recommend. You will find me using it over and over again in the pages that follow. If you happen to be one who from time to time finds yourself faced with unpaid bills and find this book sufficiently interesting and of some help; if you happen to be someone who is thinking of entering the collection industry and find this book to be filled with some good advice; if you are already working in the industry and find in the following pages some hope when you have become disenchanted with the daily routine around a collection agency, and if somehow I have been able to enhance the image of the professional collector my efforts will have been worthwhile.

Miami, Florida, 1989

About the Sketches

By the end of the second week of work in the collection agency, I was filled with a new and fresh appreciation for the often-heard statement that the difference between tragedy and humor is hairline thin. Since then, I have been involved in many situations during the workday that for me have the dual qualities of being both cataclysmic and funny.

For more than three decades I have searched for anyone who had not only the artistic ability but was willing to translate my experience into sketches. To date, three women have come to my rescue. (There have been no male volunteers.) The first is Constance Bailey, an illustrator of children's books who had come to Florida with her sister Ethel. She was a commercial artist with a local department store when her sister became our bookkeeper for a period that included two of my birthdays. On each of these occasions, Connie handed me sketches #1 and #2.

The second is Penney Chandler, who worked for one of clients until she decided to raise a family. One day she called me and asked for permission to sit in our office whenever she got tired of waiting for the Blessed Event! Eventually she presented her husband with a beautiful baby and me with sketch #3.

The third is Alesa Gambrell, who had to be coaxed and cajoled, but finally agreed to complete the project. The fact that she happens to be my daughter, of course, makes me one proud papa.

I can never thank these three women enough. Whenever that rare moment of depression is on the horizon I need only turn my eyes to their creations and I'm smiling again.

You can't get blood out of a turnip

Chapter 1
Answered: One Lingering Question

I want to apologize to all those both in and out of the collection industry who over the past three decades have asked me, "What's a nice guy like you doing in the collection business?" without receiving my reply. I'm finally getting around to it now.

A simple "Just trying to make a living" would have sufficed if I hadn't sensed two subtle inferences posed by the questions that must be addressed; first, that "nice guys" don't go into the collection business and, second, that the collection business is not a bona fide one. No one ever says to a judge, "What's a nice guy like you doing, sitting on the bench?", or to an engineer, "What's a nice guy like you doing building skyscrapers?" The truth is that some of the warmest, most sincere capable helpful man and women are employed in the collection agencies, and have a significant role to play in the business community – just ask our clients.

That said, the proper answer to the question lies in the events that were taking place as we entered the second quarter of this century, and their impact upon my life. I'm not at all sentimental about the past. For me the best of all times is today with its experiences, opportunities and challenges. So, that particular time in which I was born was probably no better or no worse than any other time.

In the year of my birth Miami was devastated by a tropical depression. I was completely unaware of it at the time but the fact that my grandfather happened to be there had some bearing on my settling there eventually. In the same year, R.H. Macy held his first Thanksgiving Day parade. Within a year, Charles Lindbergh would make his historic flight across the Atlantic and within three years on a street called Wall in New York City another kind of depression was to change the course of American history – if not the entire world.

I was one of the children of the Great Depression, growing up during the Roosevelt years, and New Deal, the National Recovery Act (NRA), the Works Progress Administration (WPA), and the Social Security Act (SSA). I grew up in the then-small town of Flushing, Long Island, New York. (Please don't giggle or laugh at the name. I never heard an indecent remark about our town until I went into the Navy!) On clear days I could see the Empire State building in Manhattan from my bedroom window.

It was a Dutch community named after a town in Holland and settled by Quakers. They planted long avenues of maple, oak, ash and poplar trees and named the streets for them. As children we were told that our Quaker meeting house hosted George Washington during the Revolutionary War and later hid escaping slaves during the Civil War.

Flushing remained a small town until someone thought of transforming a waste dump into the World's Fair in 1939. On warm summer nights when the wind was blowing to the east I not only heard the music coming from the Fair but also smelled the garbage buried beneath the pavilions.

To this very young boy, election eve of Franklin Delano Roosevelt's second term seemed more like New Year's Eve in Times Square. Crowds were gathered everywhere to hear the election returns. A band was playing "Happy Days are Here Again" and some people were singing "We're in the Money," although I didn't see any. I was in the crowd that lined Main Street sometime later when Roosevelt's motorcade came through Flushing and as I stretched to catch a glimpse of him I wondered if he had been elected for life.

In retrospect, we did remarkably well in those days considering the fact that we did without television, credit cards, and computers. Instead, we relied on radio, the printed word, Hollywood musicals, live big bands, heavyweight musical composers in Tin Pan Alley, the Broadway musical stage, and a long line of vocalists who helped us to sing and dance our way out of the blues.

It was a time when people hung a framed picture of FDR in a position of prominence in their homes, when it was fashionable to be patriotic, when the differences between right and wrong seemed to be clearer, and when the words "honor" and "shame" were charged with meaning. Honesty was not only taught in school but by the proprietor of our local candy store. We children would tell him how much money we had and he would tell us how many pieces of candy we could get. Then, one at a time, we were told to pick out our candy from behind the glass cases. When we were done he could pat our pockets or purses as if he was checking to make sure we hadn't cheated. Anyone who entertained any idea of cheating soon changed his or her mind.

It was a time of simple pleasures, or troubles, for us children. One day while playing with a water pistol, I targeted the right flank of a Borden dairy van horse chewing breakfast from his oat bag as the milkman was making deliveries. When the water hit the horse, he and the van moved to the center of Main Street where he sat down on the trolley car tracks. Shortly, two trolley cars came from opposite directions and traffic was snarled for a long time. A few pedestrians were amused, but most of the people involved were angry and I was humiliated. That was the last of my water pistol.

One of my early playmates, a relative of Eddie Cantor, gave me a violin that once belonged to the comedian-actor. I took violin lessons for as long as it took for the teacher to conclude that there was no talent for this instrument hidden within me. I also attended the W.P.A. art classes available after school with my best friend's brother. His talent was discovered in one of these classes and he went on to become one of the country's leading advertising executives. Some of his works are displayed in the Metropolitan Museum of Modern Art. The W.P.A. also provided very inexpensive lunches to us school children. To this day I cannot look at peanut butter or jelly without conjuring up memories of that daily lunch of tomato soup, a peanut butter and jelly sandwich, milk and sugar wafer cookie dipped in chocolate and topped with sprinkles.

From my earliest recollections I wanted to be a doctor when I grew up. I not only liked people but I was sensitive to their illnesses and thought it would be great to spend my life trying to cure the sick. I especially liked biology and did well in the other science courses as well. Once I found a turtle and had every intention of dissecting it, even down to purchasing a can of ether at the drug store. What a great disappointment it was when I was unable to remove the animal's shell.

When the graduating class of Public School 20, in January, 1940, promised to present the school with a mural depicting MAN'S ADVANCEMENT FROM CAVE MAN TO THE PRESENT I eagerly volunteered to paint the scenes dealing with medical advances and discoveries. I went through every book I could find in the Flushing library on the subject for information and sketches, then went to every doctor's office for literature, and finally asked all the pharmacists for whatever information they could furnish me. There were at least a dozen students working on this project that was completed on time and proudly received and displayed by the principal. I often wonder if any of the students working on the mural went on to become artists, and whether P.S. 20 is still standing? And whatever became of that mural?

Some of my friends eventually entered law, medicine, engineering and business. Herbert Kaplow became a television network correspondent and one ever-funny, always-joking friend who went on the stage assuming the name Will Jordan. Will holds the distinction of being one of the earliest and best impersonators of Ed Sullivan. At least Ed Sullivan must have thought so, since Will was a frequent guest on Sullivan's television show.

Life at Flushing High School during the 1940's was rather normal despite the fact that Hitler and Mussolini were tearing Europe apart. As teenagers we held weekly "Butt and Can Dances," the price of admission to which was a package of cigarettes and a can of food. The proceeds went to our armed forces in Europe. I became an air raid warden as we prepared for the possibility of an attack. We wardens had keys to shut off the street lights and during practice air raids we had to make sure people turned off all lights. Even the top portions of automobile headlights were painted black.

On Sunday morning, December 7, 1941, I did not fully understand the implications of the Pearl Harbor attack as President Roosevelt addressed the nation, but I was ready to enlist on Monday morning, December 8. However, the Army had rules against 15-year-old boys joining the infantry, so I went on to finish high school instead. At graduation in January, 1944, I was surprised to learn that I was the recipient of the Bausch and Lomb Honorary Science Medal, awarded for the highest grades in science over the four years. This honor would figure highly in any interview for medical school.

I entered the freshman class of the University College of Arts & Science of New York University as a pre-med student with a minor in sociology. At the end of the first semester, I turned 18 and received permission from my parents to enlist in the U.S. Navy Hospital Corps. After boot camp in Bainbridge, Maryland, I was off to Hospital Corpsmen's School. By the time I finished the course, the heaviest casualties from the Pacific fighting were being flown to east coast hospitals, so I went to work there rather than going to sea.

While it is amusing to me now, at the time it was frustrating to be in the U.S. Navy, yet never leaving land. "Never" isn't entirely correct, however, since one day in boot camp we were practicing sanding oars with sand and canvas in an oversized row boat and we "put to sea." It was so foggy that day that we couldn't see the water but we were told it was the Chesapeake Bay.

I spent the next two years assisting the doctor son of a U.S. senator run an emergency room for officers' families, serving as corpsman in charge of a venereal disease ward and finally assisting our chief of surgery in the operating room. The war was winding down and the surgeon was looking for practice with a scarcity of patients. I combed the wards for any volunteers and served as operating room instrument nurse during the surgery.

My honorable discharge from the Navy came with an Admiral's recommendation for my "wings" as a flying corpsman. One day we were expecting the Admiral's inspection at the hospital and everyone was looking for places to store extra gear. I had the bright idea to store everything in the eaves above the ward. Just as they lifted me into the eaves with two large sea bags filled with gear, the Admiral arrived earlier than expected. I was making my way on two 1 x 7 inch pieces of lumber just above him when I made the wrong step and came crashing through the ceiling with two sea bags wrapped around my neck. I landed at his feet, and hence, the award.

Whenever you step out of the audience and on to the stage, you run the risk of being disillusioned. I suspect it happened to me during my work in the field of medicine. I have never lost my respect for the profession, but the politics of it, the reasons for the day-to-day decisions, and the priorities changed my focus, so when I was ready to resume my education, I changed my major to sociology and graduated with a B.A. degree in the class of 1949.

The City of New York needed investigators for its Welfare Department, and I was thrilled to go to work. But first I went back to school for six weeks where I learned a discipline that would become invaluable to me later on – skiptracing, the art of locating missing people, missing information or missing assets. While most applicants for public assistance had legitimate needs, there were those individuals who hid their assets or disposed of them and then asked taxpayers to support them. My responsibility, among other things, was to locate these hidden assets or missing relatives who could contribute support, since at the time the laws of New York State held that even grandchildren could be required to contribute support to a grandparent before that individual could receive public funds.

Likewise, the law did not consider a telephone as a necessity and before an individual was given public funds he or she had to relinquish the phone, giving Bell telephone installers reason to wonder why there were so many requests for installation in closets. During numerous home interviews with recipients of public welfare, I heard the ring, but recipients denied there was a phone in the house.

After working my caseload during the day, I attended graduate school at the Washington Square branch of New York University, intending to get my Master's degree in Sociology. Several people I met while attending these classes could have had an impact on my final career choice. I found that not all of the Warner brothers had gone to Hollywood, California – the head professor of the sociology department was one of the Warner brothers who went into academics. While I considered his suggestion to pursue a career in teaching sociology on the college level, I also explored the possibilities in parole and probation on the federal level, because two of my fellow students were the warden of Sing Sing Prison and the head of the Department of Corrections of New Jersey. They encouraged me especially because there was a desperate lack of qualified people in those areas.

While the duties of caseworkers took us beyond the normal work hours, the city of New York did not pay overtime, but did grant us time off instead. This gave me the opportunity to have an extended holiday for Christmas, 1949, and I decided to spend it with my grandparents in Miami. So on December 24 I found myself in the middle of a snowstorm, waiting for a flight to Miami. I was not aware that this experience was about to change my life.

If you have never traded a midnight snowstorm for a balmy tropical dawn you might have some trouble understanding my feelings of awe as I deplaned in Miami on Christmas morning. The temperature was in the low seventies and the sky was a deep shade of blue, and amazingly clear. In the west, the stars were still twinkling like the lights of the city I had left only hours before. In the east, the sun was about to ascend on the horizon. It seemed as if a huge curtain was rising, announcing the beginning of a new day. I could smell the freshness that the surrounding water lent to this Oceanside town.

As Adele and Alfred Warren Royal, my grandparents, drove us home, we first traveled south on LeJeune Road to Coral Gables, and then turned left onto a wide boulevard that was the business district. The streets were extremely clean and the buildings painted light pastel colors of pink, tan and white. As I glanced at a sign reading "Miracle Mile," I could hear myself thinking that it certainly was. My eyes were drawn to the stately palms, the gnarled banyan trees with their roots struggling to clutch the earth, the bright hibiscus in salmon, yellow, and pink and the multi-colored crotons. They all seemed to be welcoming me to my own personal Shan-gri-la.

Before Al put the key in the front door I had already decided that regardless of what line of work I entered, it would be in this city. This was the beginning of the two great love affairs in my life that not only have lasted for nearly four decades but have grown in intensity during that period as well.

My grandparents, who had always insisted that I call them by their first names, were unique folks. Al had gone to work for the R.G. Dun Co, (later to become Dun & Bradstreet) before finishing grade school. Prior to enactment of child labor laws, this firm hired youngsters to write credit reports in longhand from field investigators' notes. Supervisors would correct the reports for grammar, accuracy and clarity and if found not acceptable, the youngsters returned to their desks for another go at it. It was here that Al learned his English grammar and penmanship. To his dying day he had beautiful handwriting and spoke eloquently.

Adele was a self-made woman who achieved much without formal education. Her mother removed her from grade school when Adele exclaimed excitedly one day that she had learned how to spend half-dollars, quarters, dimes, nickels and pennies. Great grandma had decided that any girl who knew that was well-qualified to run a household, and that's just what Adele did from that day on, taking care of seven brothers and sisters. She was a fine seamstress who thought in the 1920's of the idea of making handmade leather bows for women's shoes, and she sold them to many of New York's finest department stores. I remember myself as a tiny child, picking up pieces of leather, pinching them together and proudly saying, "Nana, isn't this a pretty bow?"

While they were still New Yorkers, Al had come down to Miami in 1926 to check out the growth of South Florida that everyone was talking about. He was not that impressed, so he went back to New York and then out to California. Eventually they returned to Miami, and Al became the credit manager at Jackson Memorial Hospital when the City of Miami ran it.

At the time of my visit in 1949, Al was approaching his 70th birthday and was semi-retired after two unsuccessful attempts at full retirement – once in the mountains of North Carolina, and once on a small gentleman's farm in New Jersey. In 1949 he was the outside salesman for Ed Majeski, who operated a collection agency called the Doctors Credit Bureau-United Bureau of Collections, which specialized in medical and retail collections. Mr. Majeski asked Adele to collect hospital bills for him at a desk in the lobby of Jackson Memorial Hospital, and she proved to be a very good collector. Al was certain there was an opening for me in the collection agency if I was willing to learn the trade.

"What's a nice guy like you doing in the collection business?" Perhaps if I had been able to remove the turtle's shell I would have pursued a career in medicine. I suppose if my violin teacher had found any reason to encourage me I might have become a musician. Then, if the war hadn't come along, if I hadn't changed my major in college and if I had taken my vacation in August instead of December I might not have become the professional bill collector. But things happened the way I have outlined them.

I wasn't sure that I would like the collection business or be able to do the work. But I idolized Al and Adele and felt that if they enjoyed it, I would too. I left Miami at the end of my short vacation fully prepared to close one chapter of my life and eagerly anticipating the start of a new one.

"I know in my heart that man is good, that what is right will always, eventually triumph and there is purpose and worth to each and every life."

Ronald Reagan

Portrait of the self-employed professional bill collector

Chapter 2
To be or not to be…Self-employed in the Collection Business

"What man in his right mind would exchange the sophistication of New York City for a "cultural desert" and give up a Master's Degree with all its privileges for an unknown future?"

This was the argument Dr. Warner presented to me upon my return to Manhattan after the holidays. I was unable to give him a logical answer. Perhaps he was right, since in 1949 Miami was a cultural desert. However, I wasn't moving to Miami to soak in culture. Sometimes humans throw out logic and make decisions based on gut feelings, and this was one of those times.

I often think about Dr. Warner's remark every time a new cultural center is opened in this now bustling cosmopolitan city. Recently, the dean of our local community college cited the fact that out of 171 different countries in the world, 141 are represented by the students of the Dade County School system.

On July 1, 1950, I arrived back in Miami with little more than enthusiasm and confidence, but it was exhilarating to be so close to paradise. I didn't know that there were still two significant but unrelated events to occur that were destined to shape my future.

Shortly after the first of the New Year, Ed Majeski unexpectedly died, leaving Al to manage the DBC/UBC. Ed's Last Will provided for the sale of the business with the first and second options to purchase going to Al and Johnny Price, Ed's long-time friend and bookkeeper. Both declined the offer. Al and Adele were ready to try a third trial retirement, but they agreed to stay on as manager and telephone collector until a new owner could be found and a new manager trained. Johnny, someone who talked sparingly, smiled sparingly and joked sparingly, was interested in nothing more than keeping the books. I joined the company as an apprentice telephone collector under the wing of the well-seasoned Joe Bunn. He spent the next 12 months teaching me everything he knew about collections with the same intensity as a tribal chief passing on traditions to the newly initiated.

I once told Joe that his ancestors must have been the O'Byrnes from Ireland who gradually dropped the "O" and finally made the other changes when they settled in Georgia. Despite his heavy Georgia accent, he could charm a payment in full from a reluctant debtor with the same ease as St. Patrick is said to have charmed the snakes out of Ireland. Whenever an irate debtor came into the office it was Joe Bunn who sent this person home smiling. He never lost his cool. I was not surprised when he answered that indeed the family had come from Ireland by way of Scotland. How fortunate for me that our paths crossed. Credit for my education must also be attributed to the wise counsel of both Al and Adele.

In early spring of 1951, a Washington, D.C. firm bought the DCB/UBC and hired Floyd Pyle and his wife Pauline, from Newport News, Virginia, to manage it for them. Al agreed to stay on long enough to provide a smooth transition and introduce Floyd to the clients, but apparently, Floyd was impatient and eager to assume control immediately.

One day soon after Floyd came on, Al was in a client's office. The secretary asked him the meaning of a letter she had received announcing the fact that Mr. Royal was no longer employed by DCB/UBC. Unfortunately, Floyd had neglected to mention this development to Al. I have never been able to understand this move by Floyd, but I suppose I am indebted to him for it.

Naturally, Al and Adele were furious with this turn of events and resigned immediately and I followed. Had they asked me to join them for a swim across the Atlantic Ocean to Nassau in the Bahamas, I would have followed with no questions asked; I admired them so much. Instead, Al suddenly announced to Adele and me his intention of opening up a collection agency and on July 1, 1951, the Royal Collection Agency was born.

This is a great country in which we live due in no small part to the many freedoms that we enjoy. One of these freedoms is the right to choose not only how we earn our living but whether we seek employment or become self-employed. I had chosen the latter.

Shortly before we opened our door for business, Al and I discussed the future. "Gerry," Al told me, "the collection business is a very good one. It doesn't take a lot of money to get started and the chances are you'll never get rich in it, but if you are willing to work hard you will make a comfortable living." For the most part, what he said some 36 years ago B.C. (Before Computers) is still true.

Realizing that the start-up costs in this new enterprise would be a drain, I got a temporary job collecting rent in the Lincoln Fields Housing Project in Liberty City, and helped Al and Adele in my free moments, doing telephone collecting, field collections and skiptracing. The very first list of accounts we received for collection at RCA happened to be against three deceased patients. While none of them was the first collection we made, eventually all three were paid in full by their estates. Soon we were able to secure half the accounts at Jackson Memorial Hospital and I came to work full time at RCA.

Shortly after my arrival in town, I joined the Compass Club, an early fifties experiment in social networking. Originally formed by a group of Arthur Murray dance instructors and airline stewardesses, it had become the meeting place for business and professional singles in South Florida who originally came from all points on the globe — hence its name. Every weekend was filled with dances, beach parties, picnics, pool parties, theatre and whatever else the group could think up. The entire cost was shared by the members. Eventually I became president and was introduced to a young registered nurse, Johnalene (Johnny) Bishop, from Louisville, Kentucky who was the scrub nurse for Drs. Palmer and Chandler, eye, ear, nose and throat specialists. The University of Miami's Bascom Palmer Eye Institute is named after Dr. Palmer for his advances in eye surgery. I was attracted to Johnny and we started dating.

The time was right for Johnny and me to announce our engagement in June, 1952, and we began planning for a formal wedding sometime in late fall. The last week in August, Johnny received a telegram from the U.S. Army Nurse Corps announcing she had been drafted! During World War II, I often heard of war brides, but now during the Korean War I was about to become a war bridegroom!

After she had graduated nurses training, Johnny joined the Army Reserves thinking it would be a lot of fun. After attending a few meetings she went off to Ft. Lauderdale, Florida, which she found quite boring, and finally settled in Miami where the action was. She neither had the time nor saw the necessity of keeping Uncle Sam informed of her whereabouts, but he persisted and now needed her and other nurses at the battlefronts. As it turned out, when her telegram came, there was a plane warming up, just waiting to fly my intended bride to the front lines.

Dr. Bascom Palmer's secretary knew the former personal bodyguard of FDR. This friend agreed to call the army commander in Jacksonville, Florida, whom he knew personally. The commander confirmed that they wanted Johnny Bishop immediately and the only thing that would save her was a marriage certificate on his desk by the following Monday. A call to another personal friend, John Spottswood in Key West, resulted in an invitation to come there the following day, where everything would be arranged for us.

So, at dawn on September 4, 1952, Johnny and I in one worn-out car and three Compass Club friends, Henry and Mary Louise Tetu and Margaret Petter in a second car, headed for the southern-most city in the United States on what should have been a three-and-a-half to four-hour ride. Two water hoses, one radiator thermostat and one fan belt later, we crawled into Marathon in the Keys, left my car in a repair shop, and the five of us continued the trip in the remaining car. At ten minutes to five we pulled up in front of the Spottswood's home.

Scenes from the drama that unfolded during the next few hours still appear and disappear from my mind like some gigantic mobile revolving in and out of a spotlight on center stage: hastily dressing in their oversized bathroom which had three doors and an unusually large bathtub that stood forty inches tall and was accessible by two wooden steps; a trip to city hall where the elderly, hard-of-hearing judge used a horn-shaped instrument to hear the information John Spottswood gave him to complete the legal requirements for our marriage; a stop at the florist to pick up the only remaining flower — a paper football mum left over from yesterday's game; and finally, the marriage ceremony performed by Rev. Paul Touchton in the First Methodist Church of Key West.

Over the years we stayed in touch with Rev. Touchton as he was assigned to various churches in Florida, and whenever we met he would smile and reveal how uncomfortable he originally felt about performing the ceremony, and how happy he now was that it turned out so well. I will always have a choice place of honor in my heart for the loving hand of help extended not only by him but especially the Spottswoods. As we bade them good-bye, they gave us their blessing, and Johnny's first cook book.

We picked up our car in Marathon, said good-bye to our faithful friends and were undaunted by the fact that despite handing the mechanic the last money we had on us, the car had not been fixed and we had to limp back to Miami.

We were fortunate to have our very own home. Only months before our marriage, I had been attempting to collect a bill from a woman who told me she would pay it in full if and when she could sell her home. Anticipating our marriage, with very little money and a great deal of credit we purchased the house and collected the bill at closing.

The Monday morning after our wedding found me back to work on the telephone, Johnny back in her office and Uncle Sam approving all the proper documentation necessary to send my wife her honorable discharge from the U.S. Army Nurse Corps. I suppose that saving my wife military duty was reason enough to win her undying love. We chuckled about it through the years.

For reasons which I will discuss in a later chapter, Johnny has never shared my enthusiasm for the collection business. She has always been a continuing source of help and counsel and while she has never asked me to give up my life as a bill collector, during the first years of our marriage she offered to support us on more than a few occasions should I have any second thoughts about returning to obtain my M.D. degree. I had none, for I found a sufficiently challenging profession which offered me an opportunity to make an honorable living, if not always a prospering one. I had also found a wife with whom I wanted to share the rest of my life and a city I was prepared to call my permanent home. Could a man or woman ask for anything more than that?

Two hundred thirty two dollars and fifty cents,
two hundred thirty three dollars…

Chapter 3
The Best Feeling on Earth?

There are probably as many possible responses as there are people who would be willing to answer the question, "What is the best feeling on Earth?"

I personally never gave it much thought until I found myself sitting in a small barber shop in Liberty City several years ago. The proprietor had admitted to me that while he wanted to pay his bill, he never got around to mailing the payment and probably never would — but if I was willing to stop at his establishment, he would pay me in full.

While I waited for him to finish with his only customer I thumbed through the latest edition of the Miami Whip – a small local newspaper devoted to news of particular interest to the black community. On the editorial page my eyes were drawn to the shortest editorial I have ever seen, but one which had the most profound effect on me. Followed by these words in bold type — "THE BEST FEELING ON EARTH" — were these words in regular type — "is the fact that you don't owe anyone anything." I read it over several times before it sank in. There have not been too many days since then that I have not given some thought to that pronouncement. Through the years, hundreds of debtors have expressed this feeling to me, and probably thousands have thought of it.

In one vacant recess of my mind I have reserved space for GG's Credit Hall of Fame. On the left side of one large wall are the names of every person who has ever used credit and has always paid his or her bill in full. To the right is a similar list of every person who, once faced with a delinquent bill referred to a collection agency, has likewise paid his or her bill in full. Standing in front of these names are three pedestals on which rest the BEST FEELING ON EARTH trophies awarded to the top three debtors who, while facing reverses, have struggled to repay their debts and, in my opinion, have proved that editorial to be true.

My third place winner was a middle-aged woman who owned her own home. She had been in an automobile accident and had crushed all the bones in both feet. Before surgery, she was bedridden and unable to take a step. Our client, an orthopedic specialist, painstakingly reconstructed all of the bones and now the woman was on her feet, but heavily in debt. There was no way she could pay our bill and it grieved her. The telephone collector assigned to this account came in one morning and announced that something she heard on the radio for the very first time might solve this particular dilemma. She dialed the debtor and the only part of the conversation I heard was, "Why don't you dial FREEDOM?" Later in the day the collector told me that a local mortgage company's phone spelled out the word FREEDOM and they had just begun a sales campaign that encouraged home owners to dial FREEDOM to apply for first or second mortgages. About ten days later the woman walked up a long flight of stairs to our second floor offices (there was no elevator in our building), asked for our telephone collector, and told her to close her eyes and hold out her hands. In those outstretched hands the woman placed 11 hundred dollar bills, hugged the collector, and with tears in her eyes said, "You have lifted a great burden from me and I really appreciate it."

My second place winner is a man who was past 65, but still in good physical condition and still working full time. He was employed by a construction company and lived in an apartment on the company grounds, acting as a guard after hours and on week-ends in lieu of rent. Our client was a radiologist and his bill amounted to $900.

Over the phone the debtor expressed a desire to pay the bill but in no way could he come up with $900 at one time. He didn't own a car because he had no need for one. He didn't have a checking account because he had never learned to write. But he was determined to do what was right. If we were willing to pick up his payments, he would call us every fourth Friday of the month and pay $100 cash each time. He never missed calling once and his smile grew larger with every payment, until at last he paid his debt in full. At the moment this man was visibly sitting on top of the world.

My first place winner was a very special woman. Her voice over the phone was pleasant but understandably upset because she had mailed us her payment in full (PIF) and we were still dunning her. A careful search indicated that the payment did not reach us. She admitted that she had not actually gone to the post office with her envelope; she had not mailed a check, and she had not given the envelope to the postman. Instead, she had put cash in our envelope and had given it to a neighbor to place in her mailbox for the postman to pick up. The more this debtor thought about it the more she became convinced that since she lived in a high crime area, someone had stolen her money. Naturally, she didn't want to mail the payment again so she asked for someone to pick it up.

When I knocked on the door of her second floor apartment, that familiar pleasant voice asked me in. The open door revealed a blind black woman sitting in a comfortable chair. Her right leg had been amputated, but she was all smiles. We chatted for a while and I learned that she was diabetic. I really believed that my client would be willing to write off this debt if he knew of the circumstances and I told her so. I have never forgotten her reply: "Would you deny me the right to pay an honest debt?" I left with the payment in full, a grateful handshake and a broad smile.

Very often when I talk to some debtor who appears to be in better shape than my three winners and yet cannot or will not make a commitment to pay the bill, I repeat one or more of these stories. Sometimes they motivate someone who hears what some other troubled people have accomplished. But I am continually amazed at the number of professional and corporate executives who hear the story of my first place winner and then seriously state that she was better off than they were because she could at least depend upon her social security check each month!

As a teenager, I was fond of reading a column in the weekend edition of the New York Journal American entitled "Words To Live By." I made it a hobby to save all of the words of wisdom that especially appealed to me and made the most sense. I still do, and "the best feeling on earth…" holds a prominent place in my collection.

"Rise to your daily challenges;
Relish life's experiences;
Recognize opportunities"
> excerpt from
> *GG's Principle: Three Steps to Empower You in Any Situation*
> by Gerry Gould

Chapter 4
Some Things my Grandparents Never Told Me that I'm Telling You

"This is Mrs. Fitipaldi of the Acme Employment Agency. I have a seventeen-year-old man in my office that has a burning desire to work in a collection agency. Can I send him right over for an interview?"

"No, we have no openings at present; but thank you for thinking of us." I wasn't being completely truthful, but through the years I have interviewed my share of seventeen-year-olds with burning desires and none of them had anything to do with the collection business. Truth is, if I ever meet up with a seventeen-year-old person who has a burning desire to enter the collection business I will hire him or her on the spot.

Perhaps I am being too cynical about the current generation of workers. If you may be thinking of entering our industry, if you are already working in a collection agency and aspire to a managerial or ownership position, I encourage you to consider committing to a career in collections. But before you completely succumb to that part of the "American Dream" that includes being your own boss and paying yourself what you are really worth, please listen to what I am about to tell you.

For one thing, the chances are that you will never be paid exactly what you think you are worth and you will probably work longer hours than you would first imagine. My grandparents never told me that — but I'm telling you!

For another, with every advantage that comes with being self-employed there are duties and obligations that some individuals may not be willing to accept.

Ask yourself these questions:
- Are you willing to work for nothing?
- Will you put in a 50 to 60 hour work week or more?
- Can you make decisions quickly?
- Can you admit your mistakes and change your mind just as quickly?
- Can you accept these propositions: The self-employed have the right to fail as well as the right to succeed, and I will share the profits with my employees and the losses with myself?
- Can you accept defeat and rejection gracefully?

Don't feel too bad if you have had to answer "no" to any of these questions. Being self-employed in the collection business is not for everyone. My grandparents never told me that – but I'm telling you!

Regardless of the work involved, every generation believes that it can do a better job than the previous one – and they ought to because of the evolutionary nature of this universe. Every generation has at its fingertips the accumulation of all knowledge and wisdom to date. The bottom line is using it wisely.

Back in pre-med we were taught the natural theory that says Ontogeny Recapitulates Phylogeny (ORP). Those nice big words simply mean that in nature the growth of the individual reflects the growth of the species. I believe we can apply the same principle to business and to the collection business in particular. That is, the growth of the individual collection agency reflects the growth of the industry. I call this my GORP Theory which further states that personal initiative propels owners and managers of collection agencies forward until they meet with resistance in three areas – decisions, judgments, and reactions to accidental happenings. To the extent that we make incorrect decisions, bad judgments and improper reactions to accidental happenings, we fail. And make no mistake – the best of us can go in either direction at any time. My grandparents never told me that — but I'm telling you!

Our business was about two years old when Adele and Al announced their intention of retiring for the third time. As Adele put it, I would either "sink or swim." I had something else in mind — soaring!

The first decision I made was to join the American Collectors Association, Inc. (ACA), the largest trade association of professional collectors in the world, based in Minneapolis, Minnesota. Then, as now, it was under the very capable leadership of John W. Johnson, executive vice-president. It was one of my better decisions and I heartily recommend it to anyone entering our profession today. The Royals, at their advanced age, were not interested in trade associations, forwarded accounts or the ever-present requests for reports, but I recognized the value of associating with my peers, so I proceeded to submit my application.

As membership in ACA is granted first on the state level, I contacted Russ Walsh, president of the Tri-State Collectors Association, Inc. (now the Florida Collectors Association, Inc.). At the time, this unit was made up of collectors in Louisiana, Georgia and Florida. Now, each of these states has its own unit. Russ was originally in banking where he became an authority on handwriting analysis. During the famous Lindbergh kidnapping trial the government called upon Russ to examine the ransom note. He later opened a collection agency in Camden, NJ, and subsequently retired in Miami, and, like my grandparents, came out of retirement.

In the early days, Russ and I saw each other frequently and spoke over the telephone constantly. But on two special occasions he demonstrated a rare eagerness to help a newcomer in the collection industry.

Not often have I met anyone who would rush to tell a competitor about a legal problem his firm was involved in, but when I met Russ I met a rare character. He called me one day to tell me that he had just lost a legal case brought by a debtor against him. One of his collectors tried, unsuccessfully, to reach a debtor at work. The collector proceeded to discuss this debt with whomever had answered the phone. The debtor and her coworker went straight to an attorney and Russ was fined. What a gracious act to call me! He urged me to discuss the problem with my entire staff, and I did just that. With the greatest emphasis I could muster, I told my staff to think very carefully before they wrote anything or said anything that could be perceived as inappropriate. (This was long before the Fair Debt Collection Practices Act or the Florida State Licensing Law.)

Within two weeks one of those "accidental happenings" I mentioned in the Gorp Theory proved that at least one member of my staff wasn't thinking hard enough. While attending a party for a retiring clerk in the office of one of my clients, I was handed a message to step into my client's private office. My client's stern expression told me immediately that something was amiss. He was holding a form letter that had been sent from our office to a debtor. At the time, we were using Floyd Miller's Form-L-Opes, a combination pre-printed message and envelope for the payment, so there was hardly a need to add any further message. But on the form was this handwritten message, "We are sick and tired of your lousy Miami Beach tactics." (In fairness to that collector, the debtor did live on Miami Beach.) "Are you anti-Semitic?" were the words I heard from my client. He knew better, but I was devastated.

Since it was still before our office closing time of 5:00 p.m., I was able to reach the collector immediately by phone. I told him to stay put until I could get back to the office. Once I got there (and I don't know how I did it), I sent the collector home and told him to come in very early on the following Monday morning – I couldn't talk to him in the state I was in. I am glad I took the weekend to calm down before I addressed him. He admitted that his note was stupid, unnecessary, crude and insensitive and had absolutely no answer for the question, "Why?" If my firm had been a large one, I would have transferred him to some remote job where he did not have to communicate with people, but in a small business we simply could not tolerate such behavior. I not only had to fire an employee for the first time, but for the first time I lost a client despite all efforts to keep the account.

Small business owners wear many hats, including those of president, accountant, receptionist, salesman, mother hen and psychiatrist-on-call. Some roles are more interesting to perform than others. Several months after I performed my "hatchet-man" role, a nice looking gentleman came into our office looking for a telephone collector's job. We were in need of another collector at the time, so I put him right to work, inviting him to join the staff for supper before returning to make some late evening calls. We patronized a local cafeteria, and this new employee literally took one of each kind of food displayed in line, devoured everything and spent the rest of the evening in the men's room — throwing up! He hadn't been working too long before I received another call from Russ Walsh warning me that the Miami Police Department was setting a trap to catch this man. It seems he had been making weird calls to the debtors and had made a date with one woman. Her disgruntled husband had called the police.

As I donned my hatchet-man hat for a second time, I urged the man to seek psychiatric help. He did not take my advice, but went

Chapter 4: Some Things my Grandparents Never Told Me that I'm Telling You • 39

to work for a local newspaper. Several months passed, after which I received a call from a nationally known women's retail shoe chain that was interviewing salesmen for a novel door-to-door sales approach. This same man was applying for the job, and it was my turn to help someone else save themselves a great deal of grief. Several months later Dade County hired this same man and put him in their Finance Department. One year later he made the headlines for being involved in the theft of public funds.

In the salesperson role, the collection agency owner has to decide how to charge clients for services rendered. Even while this is being written, a controversy is brewing in another industry over an "innovative" approach to billing. Recently on NBC's "Today" show two publicists were discussing the pros and cons of the "contingent fee." Traditionally, members of that industry charge their clients for actual work done, regardless of success or failure. One of the two was now charging his clients only if he succeeded in placing their story in the media. Well, the collection industry has always had the contingent fee as its principal source of income. Our agreement with our clients has been to charge them only a percentage if we collect – no collection, no charge.

Thirty-six years ago, the minimum fee on a sliding scale was 25%. It rose to 33-1/3% and eventually to 50%. The logic was that no client would turn out accounts for collection if the fee ever rose above 50%. As the cost of living rose, those of us in the industry felt that we could always make a good living on the contingent rate because of the size of the accounts referred to us increased too, along with inflation.

Computerization has enabled us to become more efficient and effective, and the increase in the volume of accounts that an agency not only can handle but must handle in order to produce profits has resulted in increased competition for the accounts. Another effect is that we compete for the accounts, unbelievably, down below the 25% commission level. I've even heard some professional collectors insist they can make a profit with a 16-18% contingent fee. When one considers that this is not a percentage in addition to the actual cost of collecting an account, I must view this trend as not only unfortunate but also dangerous, especially since the actual cost of operating a collection agency is continuing to rise with no sign of leveling off or falling.

My office Cost of Operating chart (COO) consists of more than 32 items I have been monitoring for over the past three decades.

During the past 15 years the figures, while not "leaping" up, have been slowly "creeping" up. I even find myself conditioned to accept as normal increases in the COO, provided they are not excessive or too obvious. At the same time some voice within me whispers, "Why must it be so?" I've observed that goods appear to rise faster than services and while a few costs do remain constant for at least one year eventually even their movement is upward.

For example, I have only moved the business twice in our entire history. We would probably be in our original location today had it not been for frequent bomb threats directed toward a clandestine radio station operating there shortly after Castro came into power. We signed yearly rental leases and the rent remained the same. At our second location the rent likewise remained stable. When we moved to our current address some fifteen years ago we began signing two year leases and each time we renew our lease the rent takes a nominal rise. The latest increase amounted to $55.20.

During the last 12-month period our postage meter rental charge had increased by $22.05, our county property tax rose by $7.53, the AT&T portion of our phone bill climbed by $9.70, while our average monthly Southern Bell telephone bill rose by $47.82. The per 1000 unit of cost of our envelope order went up $3.00. I must commend the Florida Power & Light Co. for an overall $.83 drop in my electric bill during that same period. And now that we are in the age of the office supply supermarkets business men and women can join their consumer brothers and sisters in watching the shelf prices rise, sometimes only pennies, but rise nevertheless. A long time ago it was said, "What this country needs is a good 5 cent cigar." I know it's naïve but how about changing the slogan to, "What this country needs is lower prices and increased purchasing power." I'm ready to cooperate.

The argument that computerization has enabled collection agency owners to decrease their fees and still make a profit does not hold water. More highly computerized and profitable industries than ours have not substantially reduced their prices. I'm sure that if you were in the market for a manual typewriter today you could purchase one for a lower price than the original buyer paid. (That is, if you could find one!) I used to believe that increased efficiency and new technology would result in lower prices but I have since changed my mind. Now I believe that all we can expect from increased efficiency and new technology is a new model. Perhaps John Naisbitt was slightly exaggerating when he wrote, "We have seemed to be totally preoccupied with the financial successes, the short-term numbers. Prices are raised to enhance the return on investment – with hardly a thought to whether the customer will pay."

I'm a great believer in keeping in touch with my office and so for as long as it has been available I have had a pager clipped to my belt. I only found two things wrong with it. First, I wore out several linings in my jackets. Second, I always heard the beeper when I was on an expressway far from a phone. And if I was near a phone I either ran out of quarters or the phone was occupied. Therefore, I told a friend of mine who happens to be in electronics to be on the look-out for a portable cellular car phone that would carry a reasonable price and work trouble-free. About three months ago he called excitedly to tell me he had found such a product. I instructed him to grab it but there had been such an unexpected demand for this particular product that the local supplier had run out of units. My friend called every supplier in this country and finally found one in Colorado. They shipped it to us UPS, I had it installed and have been delighted with its performance. About a month after I began using mine, my friend had another request for the same unit, called the same supplier and received it the same way. He noticed that the price had come down by $100. What a bargain! WRONG! As he programmed this unit he had problem after problem. And once it was in use it wouldn't function properly. It looked exactly like mine but something was wrong. He called the supplier and was told the newer unit was 5 watts while mine was 4 watts. If he wanted one like mine the price (in one month) had risen $100. At this writing it appears that the latest technology bears the higher price.

Largely because of the contingent fee, our industry in general has not been known for paying high salaries, simply because the industry in general has not been a highly profitable one. I believe that until such time as our industry can devise a more equitable fee schedule for actual work done, and comes closer to charging our clients for the actual cost plus a fair profit, we will continue to have difficulty in attracting the kind of personnel we sorely need. As of now, our clients are not paying us for our work — only for our success. My grandparents never told me this — but I'm telling you.

As an owner of a collection agency you set your own hours of work, of course. There are few industries or professions that demand as much detail for every transaction as ours, consequently it has been my experience over the past three decades that 40 hours per week are just not enough time to do all the work that is required of me. My day begins at 5 A.M. and I usually put in 2 hours of work at home before I leave for the office. Johnny and I frequently find ourselves at the office until after 8 P.M. I do not consider myself a workaholic because I'm not that crazy about working. I enjoy our home and would much prefer to be away from the office but the work must be finished.

When you work in an industry where the cost meter is continually running and your income depends on your ability to collect a dollar, you had better learn how to make decisions fast if you intend to survive. I am not at all suggesting that only professional collectors have developed skills for making decisions quickly on all aspects of business. In any endeavor the successful must learn this skill. That goes especially, however, foe the telephone collector who is talking to a debtor and who may fail to collect the payment in full (PIF) because of a word, a phrase, an inflection or an inability to listen. It also applies in our business to a manager or owner when he or she is considering sales, personnel, client relations, collection procedures or purchasing.

No one in our industry is going to make the right decisions all the time. We must learn not only to admit our mistakes but remain flexible enough to make proper corrections and get on with business.

Mergers, multiple offices and transfer of ownership is now commonplace in the collection industry but I was only bitten once by this bug. The experience was traumatic but the cure was complete. I became friendly with an agency owner outside of Miami. I admired his drive and his plans for expansion. His experience was in an area where there was little to no competition and he was eager to enter the South Florida market. However, he was timid about meeting the competition alone. We not only got along very well, but our wives enjoyed each others' company and our children were compatible, too. For these reasons I agreed to explore the possibility of a merger and we proceeded cautiously. But there were events happening elsewhere that would eventually affect such a merger.

While the negotiations were proceeding, the collection supervisor in a hospital we represented left her position suddenly when her husband unexpectedly passed away. She was replaced by a friend of my intended partner. It took a debtor to inform me that I no longer

Chapter 4: Some Things my Grandparents Never Told Me that I'm Telling You • 43

represented the hospital. My client didn't speak up, nor did my intended partner. Had he said to me, "Gerry, you know how aggressive I am and to prove it to you I have just taken your client away from you," I probably would have replied, "You're right. Now let's get on with the talks!" But under the circumstances I felt that if the two of us could not be completely honest and above-board with each other before the merger, we certainly couldn't expect anything better after the merger. The sad part of it all is that a friendship went down the drain. The two of us have not been in the same company since that day nor has one word been exchanged between us since.

Johnny has always been as protective of me as Nancy Reagan is to the President. When anyone says or writes anything that isn't complimentary she is very upset. This particular incident completely turned her off to any social intercourse with our fellow collectors and no matter how hard I have tried to convince her that this was an isolated experience, she will not become involved in industry events.

Through the years I have detected an ever-growing interest on the part of telephone collectors to share in the profits of their companies. That is a healthy development because it provides the needed incentive to increase production. But, nowhere can I find any willingness to share in the expenses or losses. I know of one agency owner who sold his employees their pencils, pens, paper clips, rubber bands, etc. He is no longer in the collection business.

Is there a self-employed professional collector who has not experienced the unannounced loss of a valuable client or equally unanticipated blow to his or her ego? But the collection business teaches us to pick up our marbles, hold ourselves erect and carry on proudly with determination, to carry on.

If you asked me whether or not I considered some of these things before I entered the collection business my answer in a word would be, "No." If you asked me if I had it to do all over again, would I, my answer would be, "Yes!" because there are few more challenging fields of endeavor, few that require you to use your brain and common sense as much and few that leave you with such a positive feeling of accomplishing something worthwhile when you have done your work well.

With all their wisdom the Royals could not foresee the dramatic developments that were to take place in our industry over three decades — computerization, expanded national and international markets for new business, national corporations diversifying into collections and computerized billing services. Oh yes, we have had our share of Horatio Alger stories and although none of my peers has confided in me that he or she has reached millionaire status, rumors abound that big dollars are being exchanged as the industry grows and matures. I have no doubt that the same phenomenal growth will continue to take place over the next three decades and by the time we reach the year 2024 I expect to see the membership of the American Collectors Association (ACA) triple from its current 3000 level, automation to continue to astound us beyond our wildest dreams, many offices working three shifts around the clock, smaller offices joining others in professional associations, all states allowing interest to be charged on partial paying accounts and the contingent fee breaking through the 50% barrier and used in conjunction with a rate closer to the actual cost of service performed. Through it all the small "mom and pop" agencies will continue to successfully compete with their larger brothers and sisters.

Finally, perhaps you are wondering how Adele and Al fared in retirement. About a year after they left Miami for New York I found myself talking to a man seated next to me in an airplane. We introduced each other and would you believe it, he was the collection manager for the medical society in New York City. "You won't believe what I'm going to tell you," he said, "but about six weeks ago I hired an elderly gentleman in his mid-eighties to make collection calls from his home and he is collecting more than many of my office telephone collectors." I told him I had no difficulty believing him because that elderly gentleman was my grandfather, Al Royal. For the third time Al and Adele, in good health despite the advancing years, returned to collections. She would pick up the accounts at the office and bring them home for Al to call. You see, in the collection world according to GORP old collectors need not fade away — they just go on collecting if they have a mind for it. My grandparents never told me that — but I'm telling you!

*"Hold fast to dreams
For if dreams die
Life is a broken-winged bird
That cannot fly."*
                    Langston Hughes

"I have a seventeen year old man in my office who has a burning desire to work in a collection agency. Can I send him over for an interview?"

Chapter 5
Collecting Can Be Hazardous to Your Health

I am continually fascinated by the way our minds operate. An event that takes place in the present can trigger the brain into recalling similar experiences in the past. For instance, just yesterday Johnny was speaking with a client's secretary. She called to tell us that her employer had learned that one of the debtors she recently turned over for collection was a hit man for the Mafia. She wanted us to be very careful about how we handled him since she did not want him coming into our office and shooting everyone. Tongue in cheek, Johnny told her that at least, if he did come in, it would be more activity on the account than we had up to that point.

The light on top of a City of Miami Police car was still flashing, the ambulance attendants were working feverishly over the beaten and bleeding body of a white male laying in front of a wooden frame house in the black ghetto, and I, from my vantage point on the top floor of a three story apartment building adjacent to the wooden house, recalled the events of the past dozen or so minutes and wondered what in the world I was doing here. I felt like an audience of one to the drama that had unfolded below me. The victim had arrived in a local furniture company's pick-up truck, apparently to collect the payment due, had approached an open door leading into a small screened porch. He entered without knocking and rang the doorbell to the house.

When no one opened the front door, he picked up a child's wooden rocking horse and reversed his steps, picking up speed as he hurried to his truck. Almost immediately, the owner of the house came out, shouting for him to put the rocking horse down. He never touched the collector, but within seconds the collector was ringed by residents from the area who beat him into unconsciousness.

This was not Miami in the late 1980's, but Miami in the early 1950's. The operating phrase that morning was not "the family that prays together, stays together," but "the neighborhood that sticks together, survives." After the drama ended, the participants disappeared as fast as they had appeared, long before the police arrived.

Today we assume that almost everyone either has a phone or has access to a phone. But in those early days, not that many debtors had phones, nor were there as many husbands and wives working as there are today. Therefore, in addition to seven telephone collectors, the Doctors Business Bureau/United Bureau of Collections (DCB/UBC) had four outside collectors. The ones with seniority could pick the parts of town where they wanted to collect, and got the areas where the chances of collecting larger amounts were greater. Being the low man on the totem pole, I got to collect in areas that no one else wanted. I didn't mind. I thoroughly enjoyed meeting the debtors in the field. And that's why I was where I was the morning of the tragic beating.

On another occasion, I was handed a collection that seemed far out in those days of poor roads and very few through streets. It was in an area which today is close to the runway of the Miami International Airport. I pulled up to a very nice home, rang the bell and was told that the debtor was in his garden, working on his plants. He was a rather friendly young man: I complimented him on his beautiful home and plants. He apologized for not having paid his bill before now, wrote me a check, and I returned to the office. A few days later, the radio and newspapers were full of the indictment and forthcoming trial of the "notorious Virgil Cash, leader of a gang that had been robbing and terrorizing supermarkets in the South Florida area." During our brief meeting in this garden he did not strike me as someone who would be terrorizing a community.

On still another occasion, I arrived at a debtor's home while he was fixing lunch. He had a kitchen paring knife in his hand at the time, and when I persisted that he pay his bill, he made a gesture with the knife that I interpreted as a request that I leave his home immediately. I did just that, sans payment.

Chapter 5: Collecting Can Be Hazardous to Your Health • 49

Another time I was handed four bills against a gentleman who had announced his candidacy for City of Miami commissioner. For some reason the telephone collectors were never able to reach anyone at home. On one Friday evening I found his wife at home and discussed the bills with her. She told me there was nothing she could do about them and that I would have to see her husband on Saturday morning. Before I left, I asked her to tell him that I believed before he attempted to straighten out the business affairs of the City of Miami, he should first clear up his own business affairs.

The next morning I knocked on their door, and the debtor greeted me by grabbing hold of my collar and dragging me inside the house. He turned to his wife and asked her if I was the man that had come by the night before. "What did you tell my wife?" he demanded. I repeated the message I had left as closely as I could and he let me know that he had no intention of paying these bills and that if I ever came back to his house again he would carve an "X" on my cheeks. He gave me a look that begged for a reply. As I left, I told him that he might have impressed his wife, but I was unimpressed. I added that if he ever made it beyond the primaries, I would be attending the various meetings before the election when the candidates field questions from the voters and then perhaps he would explain why he would not pay these bills. He never did pay the bills, and his political career was short-lived.

At one time we were doing a specialized skiptracing service for a furniture company — they wanted us to verify the location of those delinquent customers they had lost contact with. We were not to collect the balance: just verify the locations of the customers. They paid us a flat rate based upon time and mileage.

In performing one such job, I reached the debtor's wife at home and simply explained that I was representing the furniture company in their desire to re-establish communication with their customers. Instead of calling the furniture company, her husband returned my call at my office just after I returned. He wanted to talk to me personally at his place of business. I called my client and they asked me to continue to represent them by going out to the debtor's place of business and collecting the balance for them.

When I arrived, I was shown into the debtor's private office. He invited me in and then locked the door. He removed his jacket, then his rings and wristwatch. I certainly didn't think all that was necessary before writing a check for the balance! Then he pushed me in a corner and was about to fight. I told him that I was not being paid enough to fight, that I was a family man and a parent the same as he was, but he was not impressed. Then I remembered the old saying, "The optimist smiles to forget, the pessimist forgets to smile," and so with a great big smile on my face I added, "Listen, if I'm going to get a thrashing, I at least want to know why." That made sense to him and he proceeded to tell me that his ex-wife told him that I had given her a real hard time. I suggested to him that I was not the kind of person that ever gave anyone a hard time and that perhaps his ex-wife had exaggerated my conversation with her, or that he may have misinterpreted what she told him. He bought that, and the crisis was over. He gave me a check for his balance and we parted on friendly terms.

Perhaps you have gotten the idea that my enthusiasm for field collections has waned. WRONG! My staff will tell you that I am ready to go out in the field any time it is necessary to collect my client's account. But now there are certain rules that I follow very carefully. First, I never take exactly the same route coming or going from the debtor's address. Second, I never turn my back on a door or window. Third, I try not to arrive when the debtor is eating; those utensils can become weapons. Fourth, I never ask anyone to deliver a message to the debtor other than to call me — words can be misinterpreted. And, finally, because of the memory of that victim so long ago, I never enter a person's property without the owner's permission, even if it is a screened porch and the door is open.

"*Democracy is...the conviction that there are extraordinary possibilities in ordinary people.*"

Harry Emerson Fosdick,
Gerry's mentor

Go ahead and make my day!

Chapter 6
Images, Stereotypes, Heroes and Heroines

The image of the bill collector — like that of the woman personified in the Virginia Slims cigarette ad — has indeed come a long way.

When I first came to Miami and told people how I was earning my living, I received so many uncomplimentary remarks that I began saying I was an investigator. The image of the bill collector was on a par with that of the soldier and sailor prior to World War II. For those whose memories don't date back that far, compare it to a migrant worker or race track bookie. This is not to suggest that we have reached a point where it isn't necessary to polish up that image, or that we ever will. (I keep a soft cloth in my back pocket at all times just for that purpose.) But just as the title "doctor" can be misleading until we know the specialty — whether it is medicine, the law or the humanities — so too, is the title "bill collector" when one considers the fact that the paper boy is also a bill collector, as is the cashier at the local supermarket and the nice volunteer who calls to remind you that your pledge to the United Way has not been received. So please address me by my proper title, I'm Gerry Gould, professional debt collector.

My living depends upon my ability to collect a wide variety of bills, none of which is personally owed to me or my company, resulting from the purchase of goods or services ranging anywhere from airline tickets to zoological specimens. As a matter of fact, my company did represent a South American supplier of rare fish and wildlife for a long time. Since his country would not allow him to send

U.S. dollars out, whenever he owed us any money he would have to instruct some company in the United States who owed him to pay us and deduct it from their balance. As this is being written one of the extraordinary bills we were attempting to collect is a large printing bill for one million political ballots. It would be ordinary except for the fact that the election was to have been held in a foreign country and it never did take place!

At one time I was a member of a community business association that met weekly for breakfast. I recall that my first meeting was very nearly my last one. Before the food arrived at the table I shook hands with the gentleman sitting to my left. "Good morning, I'm Gerry Gould," I said. He gave me his name in a warm and friendly return. "What line are you in?" I continued. "I'm an attorney, and you?"

If I had said I was employed by the State of Florida's Raiford Prison to pull the switch that electrocutes the condemned prisoners I probably would have received a warmer response than when I said, "I'm a professional debt collector." Nothing but silence from that man. I wanted to keep the conversation alive so I asked him where his office was located. I got a succinct but chilly answer; nothing else.

"And do you specialize in a particular type of law?"

"No." He soon sensed that I sensed how awkward the situation had become and so he finally struggled out these words. "They're always hopping on you guys for harassing people, aren't they? I've even had a few of you collectors call me at the office and you're always so belligerent."

One of the benefits resulting from membership in a national trade association is the ability to identify with others in your field regardless of where they are located. I have always been extremely proud of my colleagues in the collection industry, the people we employ and the work we do. Therefore I was determined to probe a little deeper to learn why this attorney had such a poor image of debt collectors, and to attempt to elevate that image. "Would you mind thinking for a moment about those calls you have received from collectors? Were they employed in collection agencies or were they employed in collection departments in a bank, loan company or credit card division?" To his credit he thought about it seriously for a few minutes, smiled at me and said my point was well taken. They had indeed been from the latter. We have been the best of friends since that time.

Chapter 6: Images, Stereotypes, Heroes and Heroines • 55

Far too many people still carry around with them the timeworn stereotype of the typical bill collector as being somewhat subhuman, unintelligent, rude, insensitive, unyielding and demanding as well as one who derives immense pleasure from embarrassing his "victim." Webster's New Collegiate Dictionary defines a stereotype as "a standardized mental picture that is held in common by members of a group and that represents an oversimplified opinion, affective attitude or uncritical judgment." All of us use them and they are essential to effective communication. Just think how difficult it would be to communicate with someone or some group without being able to conjure up an image of the individual or group.

I have developed a theory about stereotypes that suggests we can classify them by their degree of benevolence (B) or malevolence (M). I call this the "B/M Factor." It is determined by: a) the proximity of the individual or group to the subject, b) the experience of the individual or group with the subject, or c) the opinion of others in the group. It is not by chance that we add labels like "star" and "idol" to leaders in the field of entertainment and sports, for stars and idols have been distant objects of our worship since the beginning of time. Our stereotypes of them are extremely benevolent. When we hear words like doctor, lawyer, telephone operator, insurance agent, stock broker, the stereotypes we project may move from benevolent to malevolent depending upon our experience or the experience of others we trust. If individuals or groups come into direct conflict with us or the experience is of a competitive/adversary nature the stereotype will be extremely malevolent. Needless to say, bill collectors are not on the same level as movie stars or sports idols.

We collectors are also guilty of harboring a few worn-out and threadbare stereotypes of the debtors we deal with daily. They are the images that are projected by two words I have personally grown to despise over the past three decades. I have removed them from my vocabulary and encourage others to do the same. If I had my way a national contest would be held to choose two new words to replace them. They are "deadbeat" and "skip." "Deadbeat" is defined as "one who persistently fails to pay his debts or his way." "Skip" is defined as "one who departs from quickly or secretly." Around a collection agency it is applied to any debtor whose mail has been returned from the given address. It's not that I object to the definitions; the words just fail to project to the images they are meant to convey.

Who makes the better bill collectors – men or women? No matter how I would answer that question I would wind up making an enemy of one group or the other and I would be labeled with some word that would create an extremely malevolent stereotype. Fortunately I have worked with some of the best bill collectors or both sexes.

E.L. walked into our office looking for work. His background was in the Law. In fact, he had been appointed District Attorney in a city in another state and had been the fall guy in a political scandal. Thoroughly honest, he was attempting to start over again and while he applied for admittance into the Florida Bar he needed work. He was certainly one of the best male collectors I have ever known. There was one particular experience that stands out. He had asked me for permission to visit one debtor who he had been unable to reach by phone. The debtor rented a room in a three-story wooden framed boarding house in a poorer section of town.

When E.L. arrived at the address the landlady directed him to the debtor's room in the top floor. He knocked on the door and it opened to reveal an unshaven, disheveled elderly man. E.L. introduced himself and explained that the purpose of his visit was to collect a very large hospital bill. The debtor complained that he was all alone, abandoned by children who lived up north and existing only on social security and therefore was unable to pay the bill. E.L. felt he was wasting his time, said good-bye, descended the three flights of stairs and was about to open the front door when he encountered the landlady who asked how he made out. "Did he cry on your shoulder?" she inquired.

"Sure did," E.L. countered.

"Well, for your information, I just came back from driving him to the bank to cash fifteen stock dividend checks! I suggest you go back upstairs and cry a little bit on his shoulders." E.L. took her advice, returned to the debtor's room and explained that he needed his job and that unless he returned with the payment in full he would be out of work and his family would be hard-pressed. The bank had already closed, but the debtor asked E.L. if he would return in the morning and take him to the bank. They took the excursion the next day, and E.L. returned with payment in full.

Adele Royal was one of the best female collectors I have met. She was effective on the phone and in the field. On one occasion she was attempting to collect a bill from the wife of a nationally-known and socially prominent figure. Of course, she would pay the bill when she could find the time to send the check. However, the check never came and Adele could no longer reach the debtor by phone, so she found herself knocking on the debtor's door. A butler asked Adele what she wanted. "Mrs. Royal is here to see Mrs. X"

The butler climbed a winding staircase to the second floor and soon returned to the front door with the message. "Madam has run out of checks." (Apparently she had recognized the name "Royal" and knew why Adele came to call.) Adele opened her pocketbook and handed him a blank check. Once more the butler disappeared and returned shortly. "Madam wants to know if you have a pen. She can't find hers." Adele handed him a pen and again he disappeared up the staircase. This time he reappeared with the payment in full and this message, "Madam wishes to know if you are available to become her personal secretary!"

Which job in a collection agency is the most important? They all are. Who then are the real heroes and heroines of the collection industry? As the matador is to bullfighting and the leading lady and leading man are to motion pictures, so too, is the professional debt collector to the collection industry. To be sure, bullfighting needs spectators, the stadium, the bulls and all the supporting elements. Motion pictures need the financial backers, the supporting players, the script, the scenery. In the collection agency we need the sales force to bring in the accounts to work, we need the typists and the computer personnel, the bookkeepers and the managers, but what would we do without those courageous telephone collectors – the very reason we can remain in business.

I would first have you know that the professional debt collectors are people, too. They go to school, they get married, and they raise families. They buy homes, they get sick and they become hospitalized. They grieve at the loss of loved ones, they are religious, they vote and become involved in the concerns of their community. They struggle like the rest of the population to pay their bills and their taxes and serve their community when they are asked to do so. They earn their money the hard way and find it necessary to budget and save for the time when they, too, will grow old.

Debt collectors are not born with their special talents; they are carefully trained. As I look back over my career in collections I must admit that some of the most competent of them were not originally hired as collectors. Most often they have come to us quite young, perhaps working after school as file clerks, or envelope stuffers. It was only after I recognized some qualities within them that would indicate an aptitude for telephone collecting that I encouraged them to try their wings at this challenging task.

Debt collectors are the front line troops of a collection agency. They are constantly under fire from the debtors for any number of reasons, and also from management when their production falls. Their tenure in any collection agency depends upon their ability to continually hold their own — an especially difficult job they perform day in and day out with a smile on their faces and in their voices, and enthusiasm in their disposition. They are as exciting to watch as any athlete or thoroughbred.

With all due respect to Mr. Berlin, there is another business like show business — it's the collection business. Professional debt collectors enjoy speaking with all people and are completely comfortable conducting business with anyone. They are polite and discreet and know exactly what it means to hold information in confidence. They are truly professionals, determined to represent their clients to the best of their abilities. Detached, they allow reason, logic and common sense to lead them rather than succumbing to the influence of their emotions, temper and tongue. Disciplined, they learn as much as possible about their clients, their debtors and the goods or services that gave rise to the bills they attempt to collect. Professional debt collectors learn how to be self-starters, how to be goal-oriented and how to leave their work in the office when they leave each evening. They learn how to treat each collection they handle individually and they are indeed flexible within reason.

Will the professional debt collectors in the collection industry please rise to be recognized — I SALUTE YOU!

"Whether you think you can or you think you can't, you are right."

Henry Ford

"But mom, the collector says you *are* at home."

Chapter 7
Bodies and Souls

Now that I'm thinking about it, I'm certain that I never completed a crossword puzzle in my life, yet I admire anyone who enjoys working them. Likewise, I never answer a questionnaire unless I am forced to do so, although I appreciate the importance of the information they discover. Most Americans must thoroughly enjoy checking the little "yes" or "no" boxes, otherwise there wouldn't be so many surveys in our daily mail, newspapers, magazines and on the radio and television.

I would like to see a Gallup organization poll on the ten most-respected professions. I'm not sure how it would turn out, but I suspect that doctors and preachers would rank within the top five.

At about the time the Royal Collection Agency was celebrating its second birthday, I made an important personal discovery. I realized I had grown up without the aid of a mentor. If you come from a large family perhaps having a mentor is not important, but when you are an only child, it is.

Quite by accident I picked up a book and wasn't even through with it before I initiated a search for as many books as I could find by the author, Dr. Harry Emerson Fosdick. Helen Beggs, ACA's corporate secretary, joined me in that pursuit by visiting what must have seemed like every second-hand book store in her native Minnesota.

Dr. Fosdick was a doctor of divinity and a prolific writer whom, unfortunately, I never had the opportunity to meet since he had already passed away when I discovered his works. I admired the way he thought and his emphasis on practicality. In my opinion, he was a great theologian of the recent past. I had found my mentor and so adopted him.

He wrote of "man's curious ability to keep divine relationships in one compartment of life and human relationships in another." To illustrate this statement I must tell you that I have spent nearly 40 years placing whatever meager talent I possess at the disposal of God through the United Methodist Church of Florida in various roles, such as lay preacher, lay leader, and Sunday school teacher. During those same 40 years I have represented many kinds of health care professionals. This is not going to be a treatise on either medicine or religion. In spite of realizing the danger of generalization and oversimplification this total experience compels me to say some things in support of my physician/clients.

For one thing, I believe that the problems existing between my clients and their patients are largely the fault of the public's unrealistic expectations of doctors, which can probably be traced back to the earliest practice of medicine. Those whose job it is to fit together the pieces of the puzzle we call the history of man tell us that until the time of Hippocrates, who was born in Greece in 460 B.C., the first physicians were witch doctors, sorcerers, and priests. Since early man believed that "serious and disabling diseases…were of supernatural origin, the work of some malevolent demon or an offended God," it seems logical that those who were qualified to treat the victims were those who specialized in supernatural matters.

During the Egyptian period, diseases and their treatment were a part of the religion and the practitioners were doctor/priests. Still later, during the early Grecian period, the practitioners were priests called "Asclepiads," after Asclepius. The Greeks worshipped him as their god of medicine. They performed many miracles of healing in their temples – the first hospitals. The patients received advice from the Asclepiads and then went to sleep, arising in the morning cured to return home. What is interesting is the fact that while many inscriptions testifying to the cures can be seen to this day, there are no available records of failures or even deaths from these treatments. To me, after more than 3000 years the public is still expecting nothing less than overnight miracle cures from their physician "gods."

I think it's more than coincidence that the professions of religion and medicine, stemming from the common origin, are still singled out for a special treatment. It is that special status that tends to perpetuate and exaggerate the problems that exist between my clients and the public. First, they are the objects of our jokes, even if it is benign humor. For example, "Times have changed," laments the patient after a visit to his physician. "My doctor used to look at my tongue and tell me to say 'ah.' Now he looks at my wallet and he says, 'AHHHHH!"

A young boy sits in church with his parents. Pointing to an impressive scroll hanging on the wall, he asks his mother, "What is that?" His mother replies, "Honey, that's a list of those who died in the service." Thinking for a brief moment the boy asks, "Was that in the morning service or the evening service?"

The ever-constant effort on the part of our medical and religious professionals to improve our lives seems to be met with polite indifference. Doctors have spent more time and money in such areas as heart disease, cancer and more recently AIDS, just to mention a few, than any other profession. While the public may support their efforts with their money, the majority of us still don't take care of our bodies until we, or loved ones, are stricken.

Despite their continual efforts to convince us to heed the advice in the Old and New Testaments, our religious professionals are similarly treated. True peace continues to elude humankind. The works of Dr. Fosdick are as pertinent today as when he first reminded his congregation that we could have peace in Northern Ireland if they were only Christian.

In general, we attempt to idolize our doctors and our preachers. That is no compliment. Do not confuse it with the practice of hero worship that we reserve for our entertainers and sports professionals. We literally place them upon pedestals and cement their feet. We expect superhuman feats from both groups and don't admit that they are human like the rest of us. Idols don't make mistakes, don't get sick, don't take vacations, aren't concerned with money and never get bored with us. That's what we demand from them on a 24-hour basis. The treatment Jim and Tammy Bakker and Jimmy Swaggart received is an example of our unrealistic expectations of our religious professionals.

Gail Chandler, the eye specialist, had a passion for cigars. Out of respect for his colleague Bascom Palmer, who was a non-smoker, he limited his habit to after office hours and a brief period each morning outside their office building before they saw their patients.

Whenever Bascom caught Gail smoking he would warn him of the inevitable consequences of smoking. As it turned out, Bascom Palmer developed cancer of the throat and died. Gail was grief-stricken with the loss of his partner; but not enough to give up smoking his cigars.

I had a client who was probably sicker and suffered more than most of the clients he saw daily. For years he was terrified with the uncertainty of waking up each day, so he never retired at night until he paid all his bills and had his affairs in order.

Another client was a very capable surgeon who went to pieces when he was told he needed to have his tonsils removed. The thought of having to undergo surgery himself was perhaps too much for him. He hemorrhaged to death on the operating table.

I also remember a very capable young general practitioner who could never find the time to take a vacation. Reluctantly, he agreed to accompany his wife and children to Europe if they would allow him to return to Miami for a trial in which he was summoned as an expert witness. He fully intended to fly back to Europe to continue his vacation with his family, but he dropped dead as he sat in the witness box.

Times have changed quite a bit and I'm happy to see that my physician/clients are taking frequent vacations as needed. No longer do they feel guilty about leaving their patients behind.

Would you believe it, through the years I have had physician/clients who became so bored with their day-to-day routine that they either got out of medicine or changed their specialty? I've known an equal number of preachers who have done the same.

Most of my medical clients have been highly motivated people. They would have had to be to endure the number of years spent in medical school, interning, practicing their specialties and taking on-going education. Most of them have been quite successful, although some of them had to close their practices for financial reasons.

If from time to time they are overbearing and authoritative with their office staff and their patients, it's a good bet that they are the same with their families. I call it the "prima donna syndrome." The public has treated them so often as "gods" that some do lose their equilibrium. Several years ago Johnny and I were friendly with a young intern and his fiancé, who happened to work in the same hospital as her soon to be husband/doctor. One day he announced he was taking her up to surgery to remove her appendix. It really didn't matter to him that her appendix wasn't bothering her. The dutiful wife-to-be marched up to the operating room and had it removed. Whenever I come across the "prima donna syndrome" I remind myself that the medical profession has had the experience of giving orders without any contradiction for more than 3000 years. The "victim" is displaying behavior that the majority of the public expects.

Finally, I believe that if the problems that exist between my physician/clients and the public are ever to be resolved, it is largely up to the public to take some specific steps to improve the relations. First, patients must adopt a more realistic attitude toward the men and women professionals who treat their illnesses. They are as human as the rest of us and subject to the same emotions and shortcomings as we are. If they are reasonably capable practitioners who keep in touch with the ever-growing body of information in their specialties and utilize good techniques and procedures, that is sufficient; they can't all be Dr. Kildare.

Second, while the traditional role of the patient has been passive, that is, accepting whatever the doctor says without question, I strongly urge all patients to ask whatever questions are on their minds regardless of the possibility of alienating their physician. It always amazes me that the man or woman who will stand in the check-out lane of a supermarket fighting over a few cents that he or she is certain they have been overcharged, will never ask the doctor in advance what the service will cost, or question a procedure, however dangerous it may be. Not only ask questions but expect complete answers in a language you understand fully and that satisfy your doubts. Doctors may not be used to being questioned but the results will be worthwhile.

Third, I urge all patients to accept the fact that while medicine is a most noble profession, it is also a business. I have never met a doctor who didn't want to be paid for services rendered. Education costs more than it did in years past, and the expense of on-going education to remain on top of the latest advances in medicine is equally expensive. Then there is the rent, payroll and utilities. The equipment used costs more than it ever did. Inflation affects our doctors as the rest of us. As I write this the doctors in South Florida face a crisis in malpractice insurance costs due to the heavy volume of malpractice suits brought against them in recent years. When the average doctor pays anywhere from $12,000 to $192,000 a year for malpractice insurance they had better think of their practice as a business or they risk the possibility of going out of the business of medicine.

    Finally, I urge all patients to discuss price with their physicians before the service is performed. It is too late to discuss fees when the bill is turned out for collection. Despite those signs in doctors' offices encouraging the patients to discuss their fees, most doctors would prefer their secretaries to handle this chore. But I assure you that your physician is thinking of his fee during the treatment, so I see nothing wrong with asking him to discuss it with you. I had a cousin who made it a practice to take each patient into his private office and thoroughly discuss his fee as well as every charge associated with his service.

    I firmly believe that the long continued rise in physicians' fees is directly related to the long period of time they went unquestioned. If each of us would only use the common sense and good judgment we possess we will be in good hands when it comes to those to whom we entrust our bodies as well as our souls.

"Never doubt that a small group of thoughtful, committed citizens can change the world; indeed, it's the only thing that ever has."

Margaret Mead

"I'm busy right now, but you can pick up the payment in full at 4 p.m."

Chapter 8
"The Check is in the Mail"

Whenever a debtor greets me with these six words I am immediately reminded of the late comedian, Jackie Gleason, and a phrase he made immortal — "HOW SWEET IT IS!"

By my calculations, if I had received every check promised me over the past three decades I would own, free and clear, a castle in Spain, a custom-made 727 jet to take me to my private airport and a chauffeur-driven Rolls Royce to deliver me to the front door. Fortunately, I have no desire for any of the above, since the checks never have come as promised. As when it was written by the philosopher, William Hazlitt, this ancient observation is still true; "There is many a slip 'twixt the cup and the lip."

My office staff is convinced that I was born wearing a shirt, tie and jacket, clutching a telephone receiver, and that I have always slept on telephone directories instead of a mattress. However, I assure you that the art of debt collecting is not a skill a person is born with, but rather a never-ending learning process with the emphasis on discipline. During that process all of us have passed through at least one, but hopefully three, stages of development. During the first (infantile) stage the telephone collector literally believes everything the debtor says. During the second (adolescent) stage the telephone collector believes absolutely nothing the debtor says. It is only during the third (adult) stage that the telephone collector neither believes nor disbelieves what the debtor says, but patiently waits for the debtor's performance. Several seasons ago one of the cigarette manufacturers had as their slogan, "IT'S THE PERFORMANCE THAT COUNTS." This is now a cardinal rule in my office.

I have known collectors who never get beyond the "infantile" stage. At the DBC/UBC we had such a collector who drove the rest of us up and down the four walls by reciting her complete list of promised payments on a regular basis. However, these "first stage" collectors exhibit one positive trait — they are persistent and some debtors will pay them just to get some peace.

In my opinion, the "adolescent" stage collectors can be dangerous. Because of their attitude they are the ones who generally lose control of their emotions and say or do something that goes beyond established business ethics and contrary to the Fair Debt Collection Practices Act.

Another cardinal rule in my office is "NEVER SAY OR DO ANYTHING FOR WHICH YOU MUST SAY I'M SORRY." My experience has taught me that whenever I've been tempted to disbelieve a debtor without giving him or her a chance to perform, more often than not I've been wrong.

Frequently, debtors will call us asking for clarification of the amounts they owe and to whom they are indebted. One impatient debtor called from out of town. She couldn't wait for the information and promised to call back. The collector got caught up in this debtor's impatience and sincerity and was prepared for the second call. The debtor was grateful for the information and was putting a check for payment in full in the mail immediately. (End of telephone call!) At that point the collector came to me with a smile on her face. We were about to receive a "BIG" payment in the mail.

There is another cardinal rule in my office — "PROMISED PAYMENTS MUST BE ON THE COLLECTOR'S DESK WITHIN 48 HOURS AFTER THEY ARE MAILED." The allotted time passed and the big check did not come in. The collector was extremely disappointed; the debtor had seemed so sincere since she called back as promised. The collector was instructed to follow-up on this promise. Problem was, she had neglected to obtain information that would allow her to contact this debtor. The original information had indeed indicated the debtor moved out of state. Two more 48-hour periods passed and the collector "wrote-off" the promise. She was not going to believe anything a debtor told her in the future. (I've often thought that our brother and sister collectors in Missouri are way ahead of the rest of us.) Another 48 hours passed and the check for $600.00 arrived in the mail. The collector, our office and our client had "lucked-out" this time.

I have never known sustained success to be built upon luck so I prefer to have only "adult" stage collectors working for me. I want them focusing their attention on the debtor's performance. Adult collectors understand another of my cardinal rules -- "MAKE SOMETHING HAPPEN." In Dealing with impatient debtors they will ask for all the information they will need before giving out the first piece of information requested.

I firmly believe in the principle of "good timing." The postman once delivered a letter to our office addressed to "Any collection agency on Flagler Street, Miami, Florida." Our office happened to be one block south of Flagler Street. It was a request to collect a substantial balance from an individual who had moved to Miami from some northern state; no local address and no place of employment were available. It was known that he was a disk jockey. I'm an early riser, and one morning soon thereafter I was changing stations on the radio when I heard a disk jockey introduce himself. It was my debtor – I just had that "gut" feeling. The station was located within a block of our office and it was a simple matter to verify that I had, indeed, located the right party. The balance was paid in full immediately.

Another time we received a bill for collection from a wholesale produce firm in Chicago. It was for the purchase of hundreds of heads of lettuce, and the debtor was a fast food restaurant chain that had recently closed their doors. That very day I was in the office of a client of mine and overheard a telephone conversation between one of the bookkeepers and the main office of that restaurant chain. I bypassed the usual routine of notifying the debtor by mail of the account for collection and rushed to the main office, asked for a check and received what may have been the last check they wrote.

Once I was speaking with a debtor who operated a small all-night convenience market. The introduction went well and he listened to the name of his creditor and the amount owed and then flew into a rage, informing me that the bill was paid and never to bother him again! I checked with my client and no money had been received. I tried calling the debtor back but never was able to get beyond the first sentence before the CLICK!

I decided to try a different approach. I realized he would not be working around the clock so I waited until I thought he might have gone to work, and then called his home and asked for his wife. When

I explained the bill to her she confessed her husband had given her the full amount of the bill in cash to pay our client and she had spent it on something else. Naturally, she was not about to tell him and asked me to come out any night after 11:30 P.M. when he went to work and she would pay it. I did just as she asked and put the matter to rest.

Fortunately for us, not all debtors use excuses. Many simply respond to the agency's first notice. But, the bulk of our time and effort is spent in dealing with excuses which serve the debtor in two ways; either eliminating the collection effort or delaying it. According to Webster's dictionary "sometimes excuses are expressions of regret for failure to do something." More often they are explanations for an unsatisfactory action or inaction.

The collector must first determine which excuses are reasonable and which ones are unreasonable by subjecting each one to the test of logic and common sense. Next, the collector must learn to eliminate the excuses like a hurdler on a track team overcomes the hurdle or like the military trainee learns to complete the obstacle course.

In an effort to keep physically fit I refer daily to a small book entitled 10 Minute Shape Up. It consists of a daily program of exercises which takes no more than 10 minutes to complete. It works for me. I believe that professional debt collectors could increase their efficiency if they would spend about the same amount of time each day, before they start making their calls, reviewing a list of excuses and practicing their answers.

With that goal in mind let me introduce you to GG's Classification of Debtor Excuses (CODE). They are arranged into five categories: calendar and topical; dissatisfaction with service and/or communication; "it's not my fault – it's a mistake;" I need more time (you're not high up on my priority list); and nonsense.

CALENDAR AND TOPICAL EXCUSES

Excuse #1 – "I must pay my Christmas bills first." This can be used from December 26 through the month of February.

Excuse #2 – "I have to pay my income taxes first." This can be used from February through April 15.

Excuse #3 – "I'm expecting a large income tax refund and I'll pay you when I get it." This can be used from April 15 until the professional collector will no longer accept it. The chances are the debtor is telling other creditors the same and the refund, if there is a refund, will not cover all the bills. It makes far more sense for the debtor to pay the bill now and have the refund free and clear.

Excuse #4 – "I'm a school teacher and I won't get paid until the second week in September." This one is used from before school lets out until after school starts. What is overlooked is the fact that teachers' salaries are prorated to cover the whole year and while on vacation teachers have the option to earn additional income.

Excuse #5 – "I'll pay you after I come back from my vacation." This usually covers the months of June through September. It makes far more sense to pay bills before vacation, allowing a really worry-free rest.

Excuse #6 – "I've overspent on my vacation." Haven't we all? Another reason to pay our bills before we go on vacation.

Excuse #7 – "I've got to get the kids ready for school." This is used from late August through October.

Excuse #8 – "Not until after the holidays." This brings us right through the calendar year until after New Year's Day.

Excuse #9 – "I have no money due to the: (choose one) strike, lock-out, downturn in the economy, lay-off, plant closing, prolonged road construction, business failure, etc." Any local or national bad economic news appearing in the media is certain to create some excuse for not paying a bill.

Excuse #10 – "I've had too many unexpected expenses due to the: hurricane, snowstorm, tornado, flood, earthquake, etc. Whenever the media reports a dramatic weather problem it will become another excuse for not paying a bill.

DISSATISFACTION WITH SERVICE AND COMMUNICATION EXCUSES

Excuse #11 – "The doctor didn't cure me." As far as I know, presently there are no money-back guarantees in the health professions. However, there is a portion of the ancient Irish Brehon Laws pertaining to health: For neglect, plunder or mismanagement of an operation the doctor was fined. If he failed, through ignorance, to affect a cure he could claim no fee.

Excuse #12 – "I didn't ask for his service." This one is used for radiologists, anesthesiologists, pathologists and consultants. When a patient enters a hospital, among the forms he or she signs are permission forms allowing physicians to use the services of other health professionals available in the treatment of his patient.

Excuse #13 – "Unless you can show me where I signed for this service I won't pay." See #12

Excuse #14 – "He (or she) overcharged me." If patients do not discuss the cost of the physician's service before they receive it, how can they determine that they were overcharged? They certainly haven't overpaid.

Excuse #15 – "He (or she) kept me waiting too long." We have become a nation of "waiters." We wait in line at the supermarket, at the post office and at the bank. We stand in line all night to get Super Bowl or concert tickets and gladly pay for them. However, when we go to a doctor's office or enter a hospital we expect instant service.

Excuse #16 – "He (or she) didn't do anything for me." Unless you see a sign indicating the service is "free" there is going to be a charge.

Excuse #17 – "He (or she) was rude to me." While that doesn't happen very often, health care professionals are as human as the rest of us. All of us have experienced rude clerks, waitresses, postal employees, etc. There is always appropriate action that can be taken. However, if we continue to accept the service there is going to be a bill.

Excuse #18 – "He entered my hospital room in his pajamas." This is my all-time favorite excuse. The debtor was referring to her anesthesiologist who came dressed in his hospital greens to take her to the operating room.

Excuse #19 – "I never saw him (or her)." Most patients never see the radiologist or pathologist and they probably don't remember seeing the anesthesiologist or the emergency room doctor.

Excuse #20 – "When I left the hospital I asked the cashier if my bill included everything and she said "yes." Can you imagine anyone going into a department store on a shopping spree for the day and then asking for a final bill upon leaving the premises? We're willing to wait a month for our department store bill but expect the hospital bill immediately. Of course, there may be late charges coming down from accounting and, of course, the cashier is speaking for the hospital bill alone; not other services associated with the hospital stay.

Excuse #21 – "I didn't know what it's for." When I was working for the Welfare Department in New York it wasn't uncommon for someone to call me and say, "I have received a letter in the mail. What should I do with it?" I always suggested they begin by opening the envelope and reading the letter. Likewise, if you receive a bill and don't know what it is for, begin by calling the sender and asking for an explanation.

Excuse #23 – "He (or she) never told me what he (or she) would charge." Did we ask what the charges were before the service was rendered?

IT'S NOT MY FAULT – IT'S A MISTAKE EXCUSES

Excuse #24 – "My insurance would have paid if the doctor's secretary would have filled out the insurance papers correctly." This usually suggests the debtor wanted the doctor to change the diagnosis or dates on the form to meet insurance requirements.

Excuse #25 – "My insurance company pays 100%. Go after them and leave me alone. That's why I have insurance." While my clients do not mind billing insurance companies, they certainly have the right to expect the patient's cooperation in working with them to see that the insurance company's responsibilities are met.

Excuse #26 – "If the doctor would have sent the insurance forms in on time the bill would have been paid." Usually there is plenty of time for filing insurance forms if patients personally present insurance information promptly. Most often, the patient relies on the hospital to give the insurance information to the physician and that transaction may not have taken place.

Excuse #27 – "I never received a bill." The bills are mailed and if they are not returned we assume they have been received. Whether or not the mail is opened or is misplaced is open to debate.

Excuse #28 – "The doctor told me not to worry about the bill and I'm taking his (or her) advice." While it is possible that the doctor often tells the patient not to worry about the bill to speed recovery, he never suggests that the patient ignore his bill indefinitely.

Excuse #29 – "The doctor told me he (or she) would accept whatever the insurance paid so don't ask me for the balance." That is correct and he did accept your insurance payment. Now he wants you to pay the remaining balance.

Excuse #30 – "I'm divorced and my ex is responsible for the bill." Why should the doctor become involved in a marital problem?

Excuse #31 – "My father (mother, husband) is dead and I'm not responsible for his (her) debts." If I had my way a medal would be given to the many wives, husbands, children who obey a moral responsibility to pay for service rendered without hiding behind a law that may free them from a legal obligation. After all, the doctors do deal with death as well as life.

I NEED MORE TIME
(YOU'RE NOT HIGH ON MY PRIORITY LIST) EXCUSES

Excuse #32 – "I mailed your payment last night." This one will buy the debtor at least 48 hours and is usually followed by excuses 33 and 34.

Excuse #33 – "I mailed your payment to the wrong address. When it comes back I'll re-mail it to you."

Excuse #34 – "I used the wrong ZIP CODE. As soon as I get it back I'll re-mail it to you."

Excuse #35 – "I lost your envelope. Send me another one please."

Excuse #36 – "I sent your payment to the wrong company."

Excuse #37 – "I ran out of checks."

Excuse #38 – "Don't you think I would have paid this bill a long time ago if I had the money? I don't need you to remind me that I owe it."

Excuse #39 – "I'm not about to take food from my baby's mouth to pay this bill."

NONSENSE EXCUSES

Excuse #40 – "You can't get blood out of a turnip." The debtor is not a turnip and the collector is not looking for blood.

Excuse #41 – "That doctor has more money than I have." So does the utility company and the mortgage company but that excuse stops no one from paying the light bill or the rent.

Excuse #42 – "When I have it I'll pay it." Words without a commitment are empty. This also applies to excuse #43.

Excuse #43 – "I'll pay as much as I can as soon as I can."

Excuse #44 – "I'm doing my best." I'm always tempted to reply, "You sure fooled me."

Excuse #45 – "If you continue to bug me I'll never pay this bill." When I hear this excuse a voice deep within me usually shouts, "What have you got to lose? We haven't gotten a penny up to now."

Excuse #46 – "Now that you have ruined my credit there is no reason to pay the bill." Legitimate collection agencies only report unpaid bills to credit bureaus and likewise report the final pay-outs. Debtors ruin their own credit-worthiness without the collector's assistance.

Excuse #47 – "I'll deal only with the doctor. Tell him (or her) to call me." Most of our accounts are at least one year old, during which time the debtor has either failed to contact our client or failed to reach a satisfactory arrangement. The client is not going to call the debtor at this late date.

Excuse #48 – "I don't recall going to the hospital (or doctor) on that date, but I do know that my wallet was stolen then. Someone is using my identification to get service." In all the years I've heard this excuse I can't recall more than one or possibly two instances where someone other than the debtor actually got the service.

Excuse #49 – "I'm 65 and my only income is social security. I can't afford to pay this bill." If I had my way another medal would be given to all senior citizens who not only continue to live until they die but also pay their bills until their last breath.

Excuse #50 – "I don't handle the bills, my spouse does. You'll have to talk to him (or her)." Very often you are speaking to the person who received the service.

Excuse #51 – "I can't talk right now. I have company. CLICK!"

Excuse #52 – "That service was well over a year ago and you're calling me now. If it was a legitimate bill you would have contacted me long before now."

Excuse #53 – "I was a minor at the time of service even though I'm an adult now. Go after my parents." Some minors conduct themselves as adults and vice versa.

Excuse #54 – "I have a relative who is an attorney (or a doctor) and he told me to ignore your bill."

Excuse #55 – "I know all about you collectors. Why don't you find an honest job?"

Have I exhausted all the debtors' excuses? Not hardly. I'm certain that my fellow bill collectors could list their own debtor excuses that would include many that I haven't heard. As I bring this chapter to a close the phone is ringing and there is every likelihood that some debtor will greet me with the words I long to hear, "THE CHECK IS IN THE MAIL!"

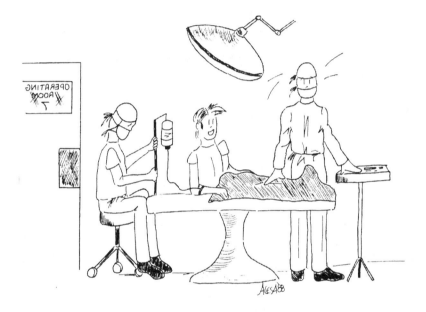

"Doctor, I just want you to know that I have no intention of paying your bill. Now put me to sleep and let's get on with the operation."

Chapter 9
Those that Can, Do …
And Also Teach

"Good morning, Gerry. This is Faith."

I had already recognized the pleasant feminine voice belonging to Faith Meyer, ACA's School Supervisor. For the past ten years I knew that when Faith calls my office between August and May she will be asking me if I am available to teach an ACA course somewhere in the United States. But this was early June and the school year was over. After exchanging the usual pleasantries when an out-of-town associate and friend calls I inquired, "How may I help you?"

"I need to know what size jacket you wear."

She had my complete attention. "Every year at ACA's Annual Convention Awards Luncheon the education department recognizes its busiest instructors. Instructors who have taught 25 schools get a gold blazer and instructors who have taught 50 schools get a blue one. This year you will be recognized for having taught 28 schools. Don't you keep track of the schools you teach?"

Up until this phone conversation I did not. I asked Johnny to give Faith the vital statistic she required and the Walter Mitty in me took command.

My first stop was at Mrs. O'Hagen's seventh grade English class in Public School 20. It was my turn to give a speech in front of the class and, prepared, I was ready to go. After the first sentence was completed I suddenly got cold feet and announced that I didn't feel like talking and proceeded to sit down.

"Nonsense!" shouted Mrs. O'Hagen. "Everyone likes to talk provided they can choose the time and the subject. Gerald, you'd better get use to the discipline." So I returned to the front of the class and completed my assignment.

Next, I found myself in Flushing High School during my junior year. It was Open House Week and my parents were talking to Miss Rubinov to determine how I was doing in her French class. "Gerald is a good student," she was saying, "but there is room from improvement in one area. Whenever I am teaching there are two classes going on at once; the one I am conducting and the one he is leading at the back of the room."

My last stop was my first class in graduate school at New York University. In addressing us our professor said, "Ladies and gentlemen, you have already completed eight years of grade school, four years of high school, and four years of college. Now, among your other tasks in graduate school, it is your time to teach us. Hopefully, with all the knowledge and wisdom that you have accumulated through these years you will now point out to us where we may have inadvertently erred."

I have never been sure whether this professor was speaking for the entire faculty or for himself. At first, I was upset to discover that I was paying the university for the privilege of teaching the professors. I had the crazy idea that I was paying them to teach me. I have learned to see wisdom in his words since that time. There is a moment when those being taught become the teachers.

Up until the time I entered graduate school, I never really questioned education. I just assumed that the information given us was accurate. Since that time I question almost everything presented to me. For example, one of the early pearls of wisdom I learned was "Silence is golden." I believe that there are indeed times when silence is golden, but there are also times when silence takes on the shade of yellow. As a youngster I honestly believed that "a penny saved is a penny earned." Now I realize that there are times when in order to save a penny it may cost you a dollar. I think a lot of other people must agree with me because I've noticed lately that very few people will stoop to pick up a penny that has fallen on the ground. In the light of inflation perhaps it would make more sense to say "one hundred dollars saved is one hundred dollars earned."

When I was in high school my good friend's brother opened a small advertising business that didn't last too long. When my friend's brother closed his business and began to teach advertising his father told my friend and me "Those who can, do…those who can't, teach." At the time I thought it was a cruel thing for a father to say about his son, but I never opened my mouth because in those days one did not question one's elders. I now regret I didn't say anything to that man I so respected. I am convinced that his gem of wisdom was the brainchild of some distant disgruntled student or irate parent. Despite this attribute assigned to teachers, when the opportunity presented itself, I eagerly accepted the challenge to become a certified instructor for ACA.

ACA's certified instructors are first active professional collectors who see the need to share their expertise with the new generation of professional collectors entering our industry and second, part of a unique "flying faculty." They never teach in their own home town or city and very rarely remain in their own state while on their teaching assignments. Their generosity in sharing their knowledge of the industry is one reason for the growing strength of our association.

Two reasons existed for me to travel to the ACA Center in Minneapolis to undergo the three day training session to become a certified instructor. First, I truly enjoy meeting and discussing mutual concerns with my brothers and sisters in the collection industry. Second, there is not a nook or corner of this great country of ours (or the world, for that matter) that doesn't thrill me.

Each state unit of the American Collectors Association, Inc. has an education chairperson whose responsibility it is to fill the education requirements of its members. Nearly 20 one-day seminars cover the complete range of the industry needs and can be scheduled at any location throughout the country. Registration begins at 8:30 A.M.; class starts at 9:00 A.M. and closes at 4:30 P.M. The fee is nominal and includes lunch, coffee breaks and a student manual. The instruction consists of theory and workshop practical applications, often in the form of role-plays. Schools are run on a break-even basis and allows for the instructor's travel expenses and a modest honorarium.

A coordinator is assigned by the unit for each school. His or her responsibility is to pick a location for the school, prepare the meeting room for the instructor, arrange to have the instructor picked up at the airport and returned to the airport after the school and encourage the membership to send employees to the school. The coordinator has the complete cooperation of the ACA home office education department during the preparation period which requires a minimum of six weeks. After the conclusion of each school ACA instructors must send in a written report determining the performance of each coordinator for the purpose of improving the system.

Over the past decade I have come to admire the work being done by the school coordinators and am happy to report unequivocally that each of my coordinators has either performed superbly or has gone beyond what is expected to make the school a success and my stay in their locality a pleasant and memorable one. Whenever possible, Johnny accompanies me on these teaching assignments and my heartfelt thanks goes out to all those coordinators who have shown us both so much warmth and friendliness while we have been in their midst.

New instructors are first assigned to assist a veteran instructor, and I was very lucky to assist Larry Poteat, a warm, personable southern gentleman from Roanoke, Virginia, in teaching a school in Columbus, Georgia. His additional insight into teaching has remained with me all these years. He also impressed upon me that I was a representative of the entire industry and that I was never to forget that fact. He also reminded me not to forget my family back home whenever I was on assignment. I listened to his performance, asked questions, took notes and went on my own for about thirty minutes that day. What a humbling experience. I have been back to Georgia once since my Columbus, Georgia debut in December, 1977, teaching a more recent school in Macon.

In April, 1978, I was assigned my first school in Lansing, Michigan. I will always remember every detail of that trip because of the love and kindness of one of ACA's former presidents and now a retired member from Detroit.

Hye Holland read about the forthcoming school I was to teach and telephoned me. "Gerry, you are coming to Detroit first and spending the night at our home with me and Carol, and in the morning I will drive you to Lansing and spend the day with you. Then I will drive you back to Detroit and put you on the plane for Miami." Hye was at the Detroit airport when I arrived. We toured his office and Detroit too, and then went to his home for a lovely dinner prepared by Hye's wife, Carol. About 6 A.M. the following morning Hye awakened me and we were off to Lansing. What a way to start a teaching career.

After the school on the drive back to Detroit, Hye gave me additional teaching instructions, took me out to dinner, and placed me on the plane to Miami. There is no way that I can ever say thank you enough to the Hollands, nor can I ever forget their generosity.

My industry brothers and sisters in Mississippi have invited me to teach in their beautiful state 4 times – twice in Jackson, once in Vicksburg, and once in Tupelo. This unit of ACA is living proof that "Southern Hospitality" is more than just a phrase. In Jackson the local coordinator planned a tour of the state capitol building on the school's lunch-hour break. In Vicksburg the entire class had a mouth-watering catfish fry on the Mississippi River. While I have never had the pleasure of touring Elvis Presley's Graceland Mansion in Nashville, Ralph Pound saw to it that I visited Elvis's birthplace before I boarded my plane in Tupelo.

Sometimes the ACA Education Department schedules back-to-back schools, such as the ones I taught in Casper, Wyoming on one day and in Pueblo, Colorado, on the next day. The weekend before I was scheduled to leave I developed a high fever and a bladder infection. My registered nurse/wife insisted that I was not going to leave my bed, much less Miami, but I equally protested that the show must go on. So, I was an exemplary patient, brought the fever down, took my medicine and got on the plane for Denver, where I got a commuter plane for the trip to Casper. We were in sight of the Casper airport when the pilot announced that we were returning to Denver for some needed repairs. We finally arrived in Casper later that night.

The morning of the school I first addressed a breakfast meeting of the local credit association at the request of my coordinator. As I began to speak I noticed that my fingers were swelling so much that I couldn't even remove my rings. I had no idea at the time what was wrong but I finished that address and went into the school and finished the day. I headed to the airport to catch a commuter back to Denver to pick up yet another flight, this one to Pueblo. The swelling by that time was accompanied by a strong urge to scratch.

I made it through the evening and through the school the next day. It was a beautiful location. As I looked over the heads of the students I could see Pike's Peak in the background. I had dinner with one of my students, Angie Giarratano and her husband, John. After dinner they drove me back to the Pueblo airport, where it was back to Denver and then home to Miami. The swelling and itching subsided but was followed by skin peeling. The doctor told me that I had been afflicted with a breakdown of sulfa in the pills I had been taking. Thankfully, the schools were not interrupted.

Other back-to-back schools were in Spokane and Seattle, Washington; Alton and Chicago, Illinois; and again in Illinois, in Normal and Chicago. I've taught three schools in Indiana, in Anderson and Ft. Wayne. Resting comfortably in my memory are pleasant thoughts associated with my schools in Sheffield, Alabama; Cincinnati, Ohio; Springfield, Virginia; Baton Rouge, Louisiana; Little Rock, Arkansas; and Knoxville, Tennessee. It was in Knoxville that I tasted frog legs for the first time, thanks to Helen Marx.

No two schools are ever the same. In addition to the basic instruction, I have always tried to introduce fresh and new material into the course from my every-day experiences in my own agency. The beauty of back-to-back schools is that you have a better opportunity to try out the new material, but the two-day experience is draining. The process of preparing to teach a one-day school requires you to temporarily put aside the office matters that concern you daily until the teaching day is completed. I find myself using the trip home to review the day's events to be sure that I didn't fail to include all the material I intended to discuss and consider ways to improve the next school. I'm certain that the effects of jet lag and the necessity of returning to the office routine on the very next day contribute to a short period of disorientation. With back-to-back schools, the problem is compounded. Unless I follow a rigid schedule made up in advance of the trip, I am apt to forget deadlines, meetings and other important events the first few days back from an ACA school.

Through the years the students have become more knowledgeable, more sophisticated and more serious. After each school they have an opportunity to grade not only the instructor, but the school as well. The Education Department at ACA listens very carefully to their comments. As a result, not only does the quality of instruction continue to improve, but the course material is continually updated.

I usually begin preparing for a school at least two weeks in advance by reviewing the course material and arranging fresh material I've gathered since I last taught the school. Part of the job includes contacting the school coordinator with a list of the aids I will need at the school. I usually schedule my arrival late in the afternoon on the day prior to the school so that I will not interfere with the coordinator's business day. Once at the motel or hotel, I like to see the school room to make sure the chairs are arranged properly and everything needed for the next day is in place. I again review the school material and get to bed early. I need every bit of energy for the next day. Following the school, it's out to the airport for the trip back to Miami or on to the next school. For me, the school isn't over until I review my own performance and study the evaluations of the school given by the students. I have occasionally asked myself which was the best school I ever taught and my own answer is at least consistent — the next one.

I have learned to use the coffee breaks and lunch hours to chat with as many of the students as possible, to listen to their everyday problems in the office and to discover the solutions they have used. After years of teaching and talking with students, I have finally devised my own formula for a successful school. It is not necessary for my students to like what I say or fully agree with me. I am there to instruct and motivate, so I'm most concerned with getting them to think and react. If I can get them to contribute to the discussions, if I can stimulate them to ask questions, and if I get them to meet and talk to the other students during the day, then I believe the school has succeeded. But it really hurts me to think that one student would leave the school with questions on his or her mind without having made an effort to get an answer from me or the other students. I have also learned to expect challenges to my lessons and to handle closed eyes and sheer boredom on the part of the students. I try to keep the outline of the school flexible enough to introduce new and fresh material to overcome these problems.

Perhaps the finest compliment an ACA certified instructor can receive is to hear from a former student with a note of thanks for some explanation or technique mentioned in the school. Sometimes students greet instructors at national conventions and recall how valuable the school was.

Teaching for ACA has taught me to travel very light. In addition to my briefcase I carry only what I can put over my shoulder to avoid checking any luggage. Many of my trips include connecting flights at least, and often one leg on a small commuter plane to my final destination. I have also learned to put together a small portable office that I can slip into my briefcase, and having it solves many last minute problems. It includes a mini-tape recorder plus extra batteries, pens, pencils, a flashlight, ruler, rubber bands, paper clips, scotch tape, glue, calculator, eye glass cleaner, scratch paper, stamps, scissors, paper cutter, stapler and staples.

The worst part of the teaching experience is the long trip home. It seems that no matter where I am in the United States, I can never get back to Miami before the wee small hours of the morning. The best part of the experience is that I learn something from every meeting which enables me to do a better job in my office.

Capping each trip, I write a thank you letter to my coordinator for the great work that each of them is doing, and for the courtesies extended to me. I recall the lovely time spent with the Goodyears in Charlotte, North Carolina, when George coordinated a school I taught there. The next day I went to Raleigh for another school. One of the students there suggested that Johnny and I shouldn't return to Miami without seeing Williamsburg, Virginia. We took the advice then returned to Raleigh for our flight back to Miami. I'm so glad we took that student's advice because that side trip is etched in my memory forever.

Similarly, after teaching a school in Fond du Lac, Wisconsin, my coordinator urged us to stay over an extra day to visit the House on the Rock. Johnny and I rented a car and headed west to Spring Green, Wisconsin to see Alec Jordan's dream house, literally built on Deershelter Rock overlooking Wyoming Valley. I would certainly rank this magnificent creation at least the 24th wonder of the world. As Jean Simmons of the Dallas Morning News wrote, "The House on the Rock is a dozen museums in one: eclectic interiors are crammed with can't-believe-one's-eyes collections of everything from exquisite miniatures to mammoth machinery, not to mention the world's largest carousel." It takes over 200 acres to house Mr. Jordan's various collections of organs, dolls, doll houses, cannons, stained glass and mechanical orchestras. The revolving carousel is hypnotizing. It is 80 feet in diameter and 35 feet high, with 269 hand-carved figures and 18,000 lights. The marvel is that it's still expanding and growing. It really is a not-to-be missed sight to see. We were so impressed with Wisconsin that we went back to Fond du Lac and extended our stay one more day to motor northeast up the peninsula to Sturgeon Bay on Lake Michigan before our return to Miami.

My final destinations haven't always had airports. Such was the case when I conducted a school in Lake of the Ozarks, Missouri. From St. Louis I connected with a commuter flight that landed an hour or so later on a relatively flat dirt runway which seemed to be right in the middle of a game preserve. I saw several herds of wild turkeys on the trip to the Marriot's Tan Tara Hotel, the site of the school. The hotel is also a favorite for large corporations using its facilities for rest and relaxation for their executives. Only small corporate jets and equally small commuter planes land there. What looks like a former hunting lodge serves as the only building on the field. It houses a huge fireplace and a short-wave radio for communicating with the pilots.

The hotel is built on the side of a mountain, adjacent to a large lake, beyond a dam that is a fisherman's dream. The entrance to the hotel is about three floors above the level of the lake.

After the school was concluded I headed out to the airstrip in a thick fog that never did lift. Once inside the lodge I heard my pilot say over the short-wave radio that he could not find the field and that he was heading back to St. Louis. Needless to say, I went back to the hotel to await clear skies. I heard that there was only one plane leaving that day – it was a crop duster. I would have taken it but someone beat me to it.

The evening before I was to teach in Buffalo, New York, Johnny and I were treated to a visit to Craig Costanzo's office, a tourist attraction itself with its state of the art design for more than 40 telephone collectors and support staff. Then Mary Ann and Craig drove us to Canada to view Niagara Falls at night. How can we ever forget that, especially since Craig admits that he continues to have difficulty finding his way back into the states?

A standing in-house joke exists among the ACA certified instructors to the effect that no one but our beloved executive vice president, John W. Johnson, is handed an assignment in Honolulu. Shortly after I was scheduled to teach in the 50th state myself I received a call from New York City. A man identified himself as Joe Leder and he said that he had heard that I was going to teach a skiptracing school in Waikiki and he wanted to know my qualifications.

"Do you speak Chinese, Vietnamese or Portuguese?" he inquired. I answered in the negative but added that while working for the Department of Welfare of the City of New York I had been assigned Chinatown and worked daily with the Tong Ong Societies.

"Not good enough," was Joe's reply. Then I added in desperation, I watched "Magnum P.I." every night at 11:30 P.M. and before that, was an avid fan of "Hawaii Five-O."

"Well, I guess that will do," said Mr. Leder. "By the way, you had better find a room since there are none to be had in Honolulu." I politely reminded Joe that as the husband of the coordinator of the school it was his responsibility to make the reservations, or Johnny and I would be willing to stay at his home. His last question stumped me. "Are you or your wife allergic to flowers?" I said "no" and hung up the phone wondering what this trip had in store for us.

I planned to arrive a few days before the school to rest up after the long trip from Miami. Joe and Liz Leder greeted us with the largest, and I might add, only, leis ever presented to us. He hadn't been kidding about the scarcity of hotel rooms in Waikiki, but he did have delightful accommodations right across the street from the hotel in which the school was being held.

On the morning of the school we had quite a turn-out from all the islands. Two hours before the school was scheduled to conclude, the management of the hotel, without prior notice, announced that we would have to leave to make way for another meeting. Through the years of teaching I have learned to anticipate the unexpected and so we did manage to bring the school that day to a satisfactory conclusion. As we prepared to leave Honolulu we were given more flower leis, and we learned the meaning of the Red Eye Express back to the mainland.

On still another teaching trip Johnny and I had just entered our hotel room when the phone rang and our coordinator, Martin Gross, welcomed us to town with these words, "I'll pick you up at 7 P.M. We will be eating tonight at the CIA." I thanked him and quickly wondered if we had taken the wrong flight. We were in Poughkeepsie, New York, and not Washington, D.C. That evening we had a lovely dinner at the Culinary Institute of America, not the Central Intelligence Agency.

The most exciting experience in my teaching career thus far has been to find myself one Thanksgiving season standing on top of the 500 foot monument erected to the memory of our founding fathers at Provincetown, Cape Cod, and then 4 weeks later flying across the great continent of ours to teach in Portland, Oregon, during the Christmas season. The thought of all the history involved in settling our country from shore to shore was most thrilling.

As I am writing this another ACA school season is about to begin. Already I am planning for a school in Ft. Walton Beach, Florida, way up in the extreme panhandle of the state. Early indications are that we must first travel to Atlanta, Georgia, to get back to Ft. Walton Beach, but there must be a simpler way to get there. And then there are back to back schools in Jamestown, North Dakota, and a trip back to the ACA home office to be recertified once again. I really look forward to meeting with my fellow ACA certified instructors. While we come from all over the United States, we do have many things in common. We are all actively operating or managing professional collection agencies. This certainly proves the fallacy of the saying that only those who cannot do end up teaching. We stand united under the ACA Education Council and Education Department under the leadership of our Director, Debra Ciskey. Our responsibility is great. The very future of our industry rests in our ability to teach the very best equipped professional debt collectors in the world.

Incidentally, I'm the very proud owner of a gold blazer bearing the ACA insignia. I didn't have the heart to tell Faith Meyer that I look better in blue than gold because I thought she would think me ungrateful. I'll just wait until I've taught 50 schools. Besides, I have solved one major problem. Whenever my coordinators ask me in the future how they will be able to spot me when I deplane, I am going to tell them to look for the only Chiquita Banana getting off the plane from Miami!

[Ed. Note: In his modesty, Gerry would never tell his readers that in July, 1988, he was named ACA's instructor of the year by ACA's national Education Council. Instructors chosen for this award must meet stringent criteria, such as teaching for a year with no student complaints, showing consistently excellent evaluations, and advancing the body of knowledge in the industry by submitting original material to be included in ACA schools under revision. Gerry is all of that, and more! DC]

"I can't make payment today, but I'll double up next week."

Chapter 10
Please Call Me Coach

Ever since I was old enough to recognize the inequity of the treatment of women in the various areas of life I've been a staunch friend of the feminist movement. However, whenever anyone in that camp cries "male chauvinism" in response to an attempt to demonstrate the theory of teamwork by reference to a football or baseball game, my reaction is "Baloney!"

You don't have to be an avid sports enthusiast to admire athletes. At their performing best they could teach the rest of us a great deal about the art of living as well as working. Perhaps that is why in every age they have been the premier role models.

Long before the world was introduced to the concept of "Team Xerox," my mother, who, incidentally, had no time for sports, had her own ideas about teamwork. She taught me, her only son, how to wash the dishes, make the beds and warm up the meals she had prepared in advance when I came home from school while she was out working to help support the family.

Thousands of years before that Greece gave humankind the Olympic tradition. At that time of human history, when individuals were known only by their first names and the towns or cities they came from, a gentleman known as Saul of Tarsus wrote, "In a race, everyone runs but only one person gets first prize. So run your race to win. To win the contest you must deny yourselves many things that would keep you from doing your best…So I run straight to the goal with purpose in every step. I fight to win. I'm not just shadow-boxing or playing around." The Living Bible (I Corinthians 9:24-26)

The closest I ever came to meeting Don Shula, head coach of the

National Football League's Miami Dolphins, was by helping their business office reduce their losses from bad checks given by fans. Over the years I have met a half-dozen of the team players, but never Don Shula. Recently he was on the television screen in Foxboro, Massachusetts, trying to explain the team's loss to the New England Patriots in the season opener. They had lost by one touchdown after the Dolphins had established an early two touchdown lead. He was obviously disappointed and discouraged. To make matters words, the entire game had been played in driving rain so he looked only a little better than a cat pulled from a raging stream. If it would have been possible, I would have put my arms through the television tube and around him saying something like this, "It's all right, Don. I understand how you feel. There have been many times after a hard day at the office when I have felt exactly like you do now."

It was at the exact moment that I suddenly realized that Don Shula and I have a great deal in common. For one thing, we both know the importance of projecting a positive image. If in response to the question, "What do you do for a living?" I replied that I was an archeologist or a zookeeper, the chances are I would hear, "Oh, that's interesting. I envy you." But tell them that you are a bill collector and predictably you would hear two vowel sounds – "o" and "u" – the first very short followed by silence and the second strung out like you touched something nasty. Early in my business venture I looked for a slogan that would be positive and upbeat. My old high school friend went into the automotive brake-lining business with the slogan, "Your bad brakes are my good fortune." I liked that, so I settled on, "Our business is picking up…the money you would otherwise lose." I have always been further prepared to tell anyone that "My business is a ball…" (and I don't mean the debutante variety, but the ball game variety). Don Shula and I also play the game to win, he by getting touchdowns, and I, by getting Payments in Full (PIFs).

One of the characteristics of the American culture is the phenomenon of the fad. One of the fads that interest me is the bumper sticker. Three of my all time favorites are:

>   ARTISTS DO IT CREATIVELY
>   ARCHITECTS DO IT BY DESIGN
>   BANKERS DO IT WITH INTEREST

During the year I served as chairman of ACA's Education Council, I mentioned to the Director of Education at that time, Tom Cooper that ACA should come up with such a slogan to unite the entire industry. He suggested that I work on it, and I eventually came up with:

PCs DO IT WITH PIFS, NOT PIFFLES!

I had found the definition of the word "piffle" and it meant "to talk or act in a trivial, inept, or ineffective way." In other words, I was trying to convey to every member of our industry that we only succeed when we play the game to win, and for the professional debt collector that means obtaining the Payment in Full. I thought that the industry could use the slogan on its stationery, in its promotional materials and in its publication, Collector magazine. I continue to have printed up desk-top slogan cards which I distribute to my students or anyone else who wants one.

Don Shula and I also place the very highest priority on personnel. His goal is to place the best football team possible on the field and mine is to place the very best collection team in my office. I'm certain he has learned, as my experience has taught me, even after you have assembled the best team possible, each is subject to illness and injury, moments of poor judgment, lack of concentration, preoccupation with personal problems, personality clashes and periods of low morale. So personnel problems never leave us. Through the years I can remember relative periods of calm in this area but I have always had to be alert to the possibilities.

During a popular TV show the studio audience is treated to film clips showing actors and actresses making mistakes in their lines. The actors, the studio audience, and those of us at home watching the show laugh at the mistakes. There is something cathartic in the process. Let me share with you some of the Royal Collection Agency "bloopers" I have made through the years. I recall them every time I interview a prospective employee. It makes me keep a sense of humor and perhaps avert the same mistakes.

First, a new employee came to me after his first week to tell me how much he enjoyed the work. He reported that he was going to fly home to Montreal to visit his family over the weekend and would be back at his desk Monday morning. Two weeks later I received a picture post card from him at the Seattle World's Fair, telling me how much he was enjoying the Fair.

Second, there was a young lady who was so happy that we had background music at the office. Unfortunately, she didn't approve of our choice of station and let me know it by changing the station every time I left the office. When that didn't work, she started to come to work each morning with her headset on, tuned to a rock-and roll station. She had missed the whole point of the music, which was not to entertain but to create a calm atmosphere.

Then there was the telephone collector who thought I had left the office for the afternoon. She cleared the top of her desk, took out several yards of material and a pattern and proceeded to cut out the various parts of the dress she was making.

During one of my ACA teaching assignments one of our collectors, without prior notice or approval, went to a local hospital for elective minor surgery and then hurriedly returned to our office for an anticipated call from me checking on the day's activity.

Finally, there was the applicant who came to us with the finest resume I had ever seen. How could any employer pass her up? Later on, when her performance could not match her listed qualifications, I learned that her college daughter was specializing in preparing resumes.

Experts now tell us that we in America are experiencing a shortage not only of qualified employees but employees in general. They tell us it is due in part to the reduction of births during the past 30 years. I am personally not as concerned with the shortage as I am with the deteriorating attitudes of the individuals coming into my office for a job and those I see working throughout the community. I have a theory for what is causing this phenomenon. The large concentration of earth-shattering events occurring during this same period, including assassinations of world leaders and public figures, hot and cold wars, fear of nuclear accidents and holocausts, hijackings, group kidnappings, world-wide terrorism and oil shortages together with the speed with which these events are reported to the public have taken a toll. Dr. Mitchell A. Spellberg, of Michael Reese Hospital in Chicago, explains: "the explosion of instantaneous communication is imposing a terrible strain on us. We are exposed to too many horror stories. The news is full of information about fires, airplane crashes, murders, rapes. These stresses brought to people by the mass media add to their own stresses. As a result, heartburn, peptic ulcers, headaches, vomiting, fast pulse rates, and high blood pressure are increasing."

At the same time I believe there has been an assault on all the fundamental systems upon which community living is built – authority and government, law and order, religion, marriage and the family, and business and commerce. It would not surprise me if future historians describe the second half of the twentieth century in America as the "Age of employee discontent." While I see nothing wrong with society's super structure changing with time and needs, I am convinced that the integrity of the basic foundation of society must be maintained.

On the wall in the lobby of the North Miami City Hall, close to my office building, hangs a framed picture of a ballerina lacing her shoes. The caption below the picture reads: "Good things come to those who work for them." I happen to believe that. I grew up believing in the truism: "All things come to those who wait." But when I see that picture I chuckle a bit because workers entering the market today are asking for a detailed list of "good things" and want a timetable for receiving them. Perhaps my opinion is a bit distorted.

Here is another opinion. "I am a high school senior who has always been in honor courses, yet I ask myself, "how much do I really know?" Our schools are not tough enough. Nothing can surpass an education founded upon the rigorous study of literature, mathematics, the sciences, languages and history. Courses like Effective Living and Commercial Foods are mere fluff used to raise grade-point averages. What we have is a country of apathetic students motivated only by a desire to make money. They ask, "Why would I waste time at a museum on Saturday when I can make money working at McDonald's?" This question was reported by Marcia Ann Kurop of Darien, Connecticut, in a letter to the editors of Time magazine, dated September 7, 1987.

With apologies to those employees who have always performed superbly, continue to do so and always will, the majority of workers I observe these days take less pride in their work, are less patient, less capable in basic skills, less idealistic, less capable of motivating themselves, and are less willing to commit themselves to anything but a paycheck. While they are ready to accept responsible jobs they are less ready to accept responsibility than were their brothers and sisters of the past generation. While the situation cannot be corrected overnight, it can and must be reversed. The general population must begin to show respect for the fundamental systems forming the foundation of civilized society despite the fact that they might not be perfect. Only then can future generations of our children learn positive behavioral attitudes and feel good about the work they will be doing.

Don Shula and I know that before our teams can begin to play they need to be thoroughly prepared. I have never expected to see a line of applicants at our front office on the day after high school or college graduation. The collection industry has not yet developed reputation for top salaries and status. The truth is, most of our employees do not come to us as their first choice nor have they learned skills we need in school. For the most part, our members provide the training either within each office or at ACA schools.

Since Miami is a multi-ethnic city, it is extremely helpful if our employees can speak Spanish and French as well as English. I certainly look for applicants who enjoy working with others and can understand the "team" concept. Since ours is a transient community, we look for employees who have roots or who are willing to put down roots in this area. Many will express willingness but are really "snow birds" – folks just here while the weather up north is bad.

We are in the business of motivating people to pay their bills, and our employees must be capable of being motivated themselves. They should like to work and be willing to learn. Not only must they like working on a team but they must truly like speaking all day with people from a variety of backgrounds. They should be mature in their attitudes and capable of detaching themselves from the problems they encounter. It has never bothered me when an applicant indicates that he or she "could never ask anyone to pay a bill." If an applicant possesses all the requirements mentioned, the chances are they will do just fine. Time and time again I have enjoyed seeing the development of my team members and the one who said they could never do it turned out to be the best debt collector. I especially look for applicants who are eager to contribute their talent to my business, applicants who can see beyond the end of the day, and are willing to give me nothing less than their very best effort. I have no quarrel with those who strive and perhaps fail but I'm not very patient with the inept.

The process by which a new employee is trained to become an effective telephone debt collector is long and costly, and I applaud all those who have that special ability to pick the right candidates. There are office procedures to learn, ACA textbooks to digest, state and federal laws with which to become acquainted and each of the various steps by which a paper debt is converted into cash for our clients to be mastered. And when ACA seminars are available we send the employees off to school to earn a diploma. Today's professional telephone debt collector is a well-educated employee. Only after considerable education will they meet the debtors over the phone, and then only under supervision. The learning process doesn't stop there. As long as they are in the industry they will continue to receive on the job training and attend other ACA schools. My teammates (I consider myself a member of the team) know that I always make myself available to them. Sometimes they learn from me and very often I learn from them. I do have an office but I'm sure I haven't sat down alone in it more than once or twice during the year. I enjoy being out on the firing line.

Like Don Shula, I have a game plan and all of my teammates learn it. At the beginning of each year, a budget is developed based upon the previous year's expenses and projected increases. The figure is divided into the twelve months of the year and further divided into the twenty or so working days of each month. Our entire operation is based upon "beating yesterday." If my teammates are not goal-oriented when they join the team, they soon learn to be.

In all my years in business I have never run out of goals to reach for. I still remember the days at the DBC-UBC. In those days the collectors never knew what they were collecting and never knew how well they were doing until they were asked to leave. My team plays to win and that means getting the PIFs. Do we always succeed? No. But if it comes to a compromise the debtor must be prepared to lose something – a good credit record. When it comes to compromise I have always been guided by this principle: while I might not get what I want, my adversary may not get what he or she wants either.

If a debtor will make an effort to pay the bill in full I will reward that effort by not listing the account at the Credit Bureau. Most debtors that either cannot or will not pay the bill in full still want us to keep their names out of the Credit Bureau, but you simply can't have your cake and eat it at the same time.

When I first went into business I often used the phrase "Guard your Credit as a Sacred Trust" because it was both true and meaningful. You don't hear that phrase much these days because it is still true, the general public doesn't take it seriously. I remember my mother showing me an R.H. Macy's first advertisement in the New York Journal American newspaper inviting revolving charge account customers for the very first time. She hailed it as a miracle because she told me that we could now afford to purchase some much needed furniture that had previously been beyond our reach. But she cautioned me to always fulfill my obligation I undertook. That's something I'll never forget. It's as true today as it was then – those who have a good credit record and maintain it can accomplish so much more than they ever could with money alone.

Try as I do to keep my teammates motivated and focused on PIFs, there are times when their mental batteries simply wear down and I hear them asking for or suggesting arrangements which I consider unsatisfactory. At those times I can generally recharge their batteries by using a graphic illustration. I remind them of my commitment to paying them a salary each week and I ask them if they are willing to take the same partial payment from me as they are willing to accept from the debtor on behalf of our client. My teammates understand that in my game plan, the game, whether it is daily, weekly, monthly or yearly, is never over until it is over, as Yogi Berra so wisely observed. Occasionally, despite all the mail sent out and all the telephone calls we made, the day's mail arrives and when it is counted up we haven't yet made our day. I have always been intrigued by the question, "Is there anything you can do at that point to turn the day around?" I think there is and my team has proven it time and time again. When we come up short, a concerted effort is made to get our debtors into our office with their PIFs or to allow us to pick up their PIFs. It is part of the game plan and it has allowed us to win many games that we would otherwise have lost. Both Don Shula and I peruse the last game's performance in an effort to improve our technique. I have always been more interested in making necessary corrections than placing blame.

Finally, when the game is over, Don Shula and I put it to rest when we have learned all we can from careful review and prepare to play another day. Incidentally, while I fully understand the use of terms like "employer" and "employee," I don't especially like to be addressed as the employer because it suggests to me that my goals are different from the others in my organization. I don't think they are. Everyone works to earn a living and the more we make the more we believe we need. If we make it in office, everyone will share, but if we lose, I alone assume responsibility for the loss. What could be fairer than that? Another reason why I avoid being called the "boss" is that it suggests to me arbitrary behavior. I am willing to listen to my teammates and try what they suggest if it will get the results we are striving for. So please, just call me "coach."

"Did you leave a call for a Penelope, Friday?"

"No, I don't have the 'Fs' in my part of the alphabet."

"I meant, did you leave a call for a Penelope-dash-Friday."

"No, I don't have the 'Ds' either."

Chapter 11
Debtor's Letters

A special relationship exists between professional debt collectors and their Post Office. It is the same kind of relationship that exists between television networks and the Nielson ratings. Both are utterly dependent on the other, yet both always suspect that the other is not giving them their due.

In our early days in business we were on the sixth floor of the Langford Building in downtown Miami. A lovely elderly gentleman who had been in commercial collections for a long time had an office on the fifth floor. Our postman always delivered mail from the top floor of the building to the bottom, and after both deliveries each day (yes, in those days the postman always came twice) I could always depend on Harry walking up one flight and asking me how many pieces of mail I received. Often he would go running after the postman to insist that there had to be more mail for him. Harry has since made his Last Big Deposit. I periodically remind Johnny that when the time comes for me to make my Last Big Deposit, I don't want her to waste time grieving — instead, I want her to rejoice in the fact that I will be enjoying my first complete rest since I entered the collection industry. I'm sure that is what God has in store for all professional debt collectors because they experience everything else on earth!

Because of Harry I have since maintained a post office box in one post office and door-to-door delivery at the office from another. That way, if one goofs I still have another opportunity to win the game. Also, this way I have a more accurate way of determining our ability to control where payments are sent.

It may come as a complete surprise to those outside the industry that not every envelope we open contains a payment. Of course, we do get payments. We get letters from attorneys; we get some payments and letters from insurance companies, and more payments and letters from our debtors. Whenever I open up a letter from a debtor I have a mental image of the writer and comedian Steve Allen at center stage. When his television show originated from New York, Allen had a spot each week where he read a letter to the editor. His first words were quite natural, but as he proceeded he emphasized certain words and his manner become belligerent. The result was humor. Should he ever decide to return to the stage, I can keep him in material for a long time.

What follows is a sampling of letters I receive daily.

"Here is the doctor's lousy money. You can tell him for me that I hope he buys candles for his coffin with it!"

Fortunately, most of the letters we receive are not this venomous.

"Dear Sir:
Sorry for the delay in payments, but I was in a car accident and had my car totaled, then I lost my job, then my husband. BUT THANK GOD, I replaced the car, had plastic surgery, got a job and my husband back. So I will be paying you off real soon!"

You just know this woman has turned things around.

"Royal Collection Agency:
It shall be noted by you and your client that his bill is being paid under extreme protest. Since this is the first time I have ever received any notice of any amount owed, I am taking this as harassment. You will inform your client that he is never again to treat any of my children. I feel (and have always felt) that his charges were excessive. If this is turned over to a credit bureau, I will contemplate sending this matter to my attorney for review."

Since most of our accounts come to us about twelve months after the service, I find it hard to believe that our clients have never sent any bills to their patients. And since this doctor did not wander up and down the streets looking for patients to treat, some responsible person or persons brought the patient into the doctor's office. After the service you can be sure the charges were mentioned and, if by some chance they were not, the responsible party or parties should have asked for the charges.

"I don't know what this bill is for so please collect it from my insurance company."

If this patient honestly doesn't know what service was performed, I would think she would want to know. But I get the impression that it really doesn't matter so long as someone else is going to pay for it.

"Dear Sirs:
The treatment I received by your clients was so poor that my life was threatened by their uncaring attitude. My medical coverage paid them for the major portion of their bill. Tell them to stop dunning me or I'll contact my own lawyers. We are paying this bill under protest. I challenge you to prove that it has not been paid and you are ripping us off. If I find you are defrauding us, I will prosecute to the limit of the law."

"Amos. He died in 1982. He is not here anymore. I am living on a fixed income. I can't pay his bill. I can hardly pay my bills. I am in need of food now. I don't work. I am his wife. I am a handicap with no food stamps yet. I was on a visit to Georgia when all this happened. I don't know nothing about it. It was only told to me."

"To Whom It May Concern:
This is to inform you that Charlie's dead. Enclosed is the payment due. May his soul rest in peace – No more pain, no more bills."

Sometimes the letters consist of only one word:
"Dead."

I assume that means that the debtor is deceased. Sometimes one more word is added which changes the complexion of the letter dramatically:

"Drop Dead."
And then there are times when the letters have a few more words:

"This is the only job you can find? Rip off!!!!! Stick it!!!!!"

No matter how many bills are sent out by clients, their billing services, or their collection agencies, we still get letters daily like these:

"I have no idea what this is about. My insurance paid 100% of the bills. Please check this out."

And I keep asking myself why the debtor hasn't checked this out a long time ago.

"I don't know who this person is. I am sending you the money so you will leave me alone. It's a shame you have to pay for a doctor you never heard of before."

"I dispute this bill. I have no knowledge of what this was for. If this is in the Credit Bureau you will hear from my attorney."

"I dispute this bill. It was handled by my insurance company. I had to report the insurance to the insurance commission for the way my case was handled. I no longer reside at the address given. My number is non-published."

Somehow I get the feeling that this debtor is really not that interested in settling this matter, otherwise she would have called us or given us her new address and phone number.

"Gentlemen: With regards to the Notice you send me in regard to the above bill I have no idea what Doctor this bill belongs to. I don't think I owe any money to anybody, as I always ask the Doctor before he examines me if he accepts my insurance. Please tell me what Doctor has told you that I owe this money to. And I cannot pay as I have no money."

In response to our notice that a balance was owed to a pathologist we received this reply:

"I have no record of ever having purchased anything from your client or have I ever hired him to perform any service. I am therefore demanding that you produce the following:

1 – A full description of the item or service your client claims to have supplied or rendered.

2 – A copy of the purchase order or of any document that shows I have ever ordered anything from you client or hired him to do any work.

3 – A copy of the receipt for the alleged item or service, showing date, place and proof of delivery.

I would like to remind you that using the U.S. Mail for extortion purposes is in violation of both Federal and State Laws. Please be advised that any attempt to extort money for a non-existent debt will be reported to all the pertinent Federal and State Law Enforcement Agencies and brought to the attention of the appropriate Grand Jury."

I am sure that if and when the American people ever demand to be treated by the medical profession like a package being delivered from Chicago to New York, the doctors will be pleased to oblige.

After receiving our notice that his delinquent bill had been placed with us for collection, one gentleman replied:

"This bill pertains to my wife who passed away last year. At the moment this service was rendered to her she was a member of a Health Maintenance Organization and this bill is supposed to be paid by them. Please contact them in order to obtain payment."

A case could be made that the next letter was or was not a letter from a debtor. In response to our first notice we received this reply:

"For your information the party you addressed returned to South America about 6 months ago."

This reminded me of a scene in the movie "Charlie's Aunt" that brought down the house with laughter. Ray Bolger, the actor, was masquerading as a woman and was introduced to a gentleman who asked him where he lived. "Brazil," was the reply. "What part of Brazil?" inquired the gentleman. "The residential part!"

In response to our notice for service rendered over a year past to his wife, one man wrote:

"My wife and I will be divorced in 30 days. Her address is unknown to me. I do know that her insurance was supposed to pay this bill in full."

Ever since Adam pointed a finger at Eve it has been imperfectly human for mankind to blame someone else for his or her problems. Why should debtors be different?

"To Whom It May Concern:
I don't need any fancy stationery to tell you my name. When I was in the hospital I was fully covered by an out-of-state insurance. I was sent to the trauma department and then to my room. I wish to know the name of this doctor, because I was not told. I will not pay anyone who will not let me know who he or she is. My insurance has paid all the monies due the Hospital. If this quack doctor will not let me know who he is, no less, I am 100% covered in any hospital with my hospitalization. No one is going to get my money. You as a collection agency just don't bother my credit. I have the best credit, do not mess with it. As a collection agency you are supposed to call the creditor to find out why and when. Then comes the Judgment, Hearing, Deposition, liens on the house, come on I know all about it. I feel if the doctor wants any money let him or you, "Collection" collect the money from my insurance company. Because I was told by my insurance company that the doctor used his own stationery that is why he got what he got. You do not use your own stationery only if it is being done in your own office. Leave me alone or else meet me in court. No more of the B/S."

"Sir: This late payment is not my fault. That was the mistake of your approach to my insurance company. After I sent a letter through my attorney to the insurance company I recently got the payment from the insurance company. Somewhere something went wrong between the insurance company and you people's approach for the claim. Thank you."

"Agency: Here is a check for the amount due. Please delete this completely from my credit bureau record since it is not my fault that they sent this bill to an address which I lived at over 3 years ago. I did not supply them that address. I am going to apply for a credit card and I don't wish for this to show up again. Thank you."

Mail was sent to the only address given and the service date was a year old, not three.

"To Whom It May Concern:
I would like for you to know that the account I am paying off is not mine. It is my mother's account who has the same name as mine. So I do not appreciate you rushing me to pay off this account. I am paying as much as I can, as fast as I can so have patience because I don't have to do it."

In fact, it was her account.

"August 7
Dear Royal Collection Agency:
On July 27 I received a collection notice from your agency and would like to inform you of the following information. First of all, I am hereby notifying you that I dispute the validity of this debt. I demand that your agency obtain verification of the alleged debt or obtain a copy of the judgment against me and mail a copy of such judgment or verification to me at my new address listed below. I also demand the name and address of the original creditor if different from the current creditor. I believe that this alleged debt is false and erroneous, and I will take all necessary legal action against any and all individuals or entities who improperly damage my credit or violate any state or federal law in this matter. Secondly, I have moved to a new residence and all future correspondence regarding this matter should be sent to me at the below listed address. I look forward to hearing from you promptly regarding this matter."

We immediately checked with our client, an M.D. and were informed that this debtor had listed a group insurance with her place of employment. Our client had been told to bill the patient directly, since she did not have a policy with the group. Since no new address had ever been furnished to our client, all billing went to the original address, as did our first form, and none had been returned. So we sent the debtor a complete itemized statement of services rendered and a detailed explanation of what our client had told us, which resulted in the following reply from this same debtor.

"September 16

Dear Mr. Gould:

Thank you for your letter of August 12, regarding the above referenced matter. I have submitted the bill which was attached to your letter to my insurance carrier for payment. You will note that the date on the bill to me from your client is "8/12" of this year and not a bill dated when the treatment was apparently performed on 5/29 and 6/2 of last year. This reinforces my position that due to clerical error in your client's office or in your office, I was never at any time billed for these allegedly past due services or even advised of the existence of this bill. I mention this to you because it would be unconscionable for you to pursue collection activity against me and damage my credit rating when the bill was never first presented to me for payment. My hospital stay in 1986 resulted in numerous bills, all of which have been submitted to the insurance and paid. Had your doctor's office properly billed me for this amount when the services were performed, the bill would have been promptly paid. Please note that if the clerical errors referred to herein detrimentally affect my credit file, I will take all appropriate legal action against all responsible parties."

"Sir: I don't know the doctor you represent, nor have I ever given him permission to treat my daughter who is a minor. I would suggest you bill the party or parties who approved the medical treatment of my daughter without my consent. Thank you."

"This is unbelievable. I have Medicare and you want my money. Sorry, I don't have a penny. But I have a nephew who is a lawyer and please don't send me to a collection agency because I will put you under my nephew's office because you cannot refuse to accept Medicare and I will call the hospital president to inform him of you."

This was for a balance after Medicare.

After we had informed another debtor that her insurance company had refused to pay her bill we received this letter:

"Don't you people keep a record of phone agreements and understandings, and read your incoming mail? Accordingly I am herewith returning the notice from you (received yesterday). Your file (?) should show my change of address. This notice is completely inappropriate; to recount our last few communications. After refusing your first form I replied in writing for the need for details. After receiving your statement, I wrote outlining what I believed to be necessary to resolve the situation. Now I receive this dumb notice. I ask you what kind of an office do you operate? As a retired manager-level businesswoman – well, need I say any more…don't bother me further in the matter."

After writing a debtor regarding her balance after an insurance payment we received the following reply:

"To Whom It May Concern:
I went to see my mother's doctor about my bronchitis. He referred me to your client for X-rays. And now a year later you tell me I owe this doctor a balance. Please have in mind that I was under the impression that your doctor was completely covered by my mom's insurance plan because I was sent to him by a doctor covered by my mom's insurance plan. Due to the negligence on your doctor's behalf I am now on a delinquent account. At this moment I have a serious economic situation which unables (sic) me to pay the bill. I would appreciate it if you would write this bill off. But I want you to know that I am satisfied with his service."

"My insurance has paid these doctors the 'reasonable allowed amount,' therefore any amount over this is considered 'unreasonable.' I suggest you refer back to your client as to why they do not consider the 'allowable amount' sufficient payment."

"Gentlemen: Earlier this year I was mugged and subsequently entered the Emergency Room at the hospital. There I was administered to by the Emergency Room doctor. I had X-rays done but at no time did I encounter your client. Five months after the service I finally got a bill from him for reading my X-rays. I informed the insurance company to investigate the situation and if the charge could be substantiated then by all means pay the bill. Evidently they found the charges for services misstated as I did. I don't honestly believe the service was rendered to myself. There is no reference to my numerical admittance record nor to my case number by the police. I have no problem paying for the service rendered but in this case I believe this debt is unsupportable."

Our client did, in fact, interpret the X-rays. Most patients never encounter the radiologist. There are perhaps several reasons why the insurance company failed to pay on this claim and the patient could not assume it was because the charges for services were misstated. Quite often the client's account number is different from the hospital account number and the police report number.

"Myself, my wife and son went to the hospital to have his wrist checked for a possible fracture. We arrived about 5:30 P.M. and were met by the school football team's trainer. It was some two hours later before any assistance was provided. The icepack was provided by the school prior to arriving at the hospital. The ER doctor and nurses were joking around with each other and seemingly having a good time between checking on the various patients in the ER. There were long periods of time in which they did what seemed to be nothing except discussing the day's events. They did absolutely nothing for my son during this time period. After sitting in the ER for now what must have been over an hour, my son was taken by a technician to have his wrist X-rayed. The ER doctor read the X-ray and the following morning a doctor from outside the hospital set my son's arm in a cast. There was absolutely no one else who read the X-ray nor was it requested that the X-ray be read by anyone else. If someone read the hospital X-ray in the hospital it was for purposes unknown to me. My insurance company paid the cost of the strapping provided by the hospital as well as the X-ray. In terms of any other service received in those almost five hours at the hospital, we received none. I am not paying for services not received."

I certainly can empathize with this debtor. As one who has not only worked in an emergency room but who has also brought family to an emergency room for treatment I do understand that the minutes seem like hours when we are waiting for treatment. And it is true that there are some employees in the ER who are less caring than others (as there are in banks and department stores and post offices and insurance companies, etc.). But when the film of the wrist was actually made and developed it was presented to the radiologist on duty for his interpretation which was relayed to the ER doctor and the debtor's private physician. The insurance company paid the hospital for the actual cost of the X-ray film and the development. The interpretation was separate and not included.

"Royal Collection Agency –
I am covered by insurance. Please dun them for the bill; not me. I dispute the validity of the debt being attributed to me – it should be attributed to the insurance company. If you ruin my credit as an individual because you can't get a corporation to pay, we shall meet in court."

And after sending a debtor a detailed itemized statement on her account and explaining it further over the phone we received this note:

"We have discussed this before; I have no idea what this debt is for. If you will give me a just bill, then I will pay it."

Occasionally, a debtor will insist they have paid the account and have the cancelled check. Very often a Photostat of both sides of the cancelled check can clear up whatever problem exists. In response to one such request we received this letter:

"As you know you requested the enclosed – Please refund by return mail
2 copies……$.30   1 stamp…..$.22 = $.52
If you are honest I will receive the above. And if you are not – well we will see."

"Dear Sir:
I do not know your client. If you put this in my credit report you will be sued."
In response to our notice concerning a four digit balance we received this reply:
"PAYMENT HAS BEEN MADE FOR SERVICES RENDERED."

Quite honestly I did not believe that this debtor sent a check to my client (it did not come to us) but we went through the routine of checking with the client and learned that we guessed right — the debtor did not send any check to the client. What this debtor was saying was that in his opinion no service was rendered to him.

Then there are the letters addressed to our sense of compassion. Through the years I have found my colleagues in the industry to be as compassionate as any other human beings and ample evidence substantiates this claim.

"At the moment of the accident I was unemployed, no insurance, no Medicare. Nor have I any assets, no car, no home. I cannot even afford the 22 cent stamp to mail this reply. I cannot starve to pay this account."

Human beings are the same regardless of the language they speak.

"A quien pueda interesar en este momento que llega este papel salgo para el hospital, y ase un ano que no puedo trabajar en cuanto enpuse a trabajar empesare a pagar. Gracias."

Which very liberally translated says:

"To Whom It May Concern: At the moment this paper is done I am leaving for the hospital, it has been a year that I don't work, because I can't , as soon as I start working I will start paying. Thank you."

"Si el Dr. que cabio de mi seguro $1000 y tanto no puedo descarto $58 de perdida, emaguese como yo que estoy disabilata, no trabajo y ucebo $244 de social security menos pueda si le mando $5 me lo puitoria de comer, y hoy uces que no tengo ni luz en mi casa. O.K."

Again, liberally translated says:

"If the doctor that has collected from my insurance over $1000 and can't take a loss of $58, imagine me. I am disabled, I don't work and get $244 a month from my social security and if I send you $5 a month you will take it away from my food. Sometimes I don't even have lights in my house. O.K."

In response to our first form notifying the debtor of a rather large bill owed to a radiologist we received this letter:

"Please understand that I cannot afford to pay this bill. I am sending you a copy of my Medicaid card from the State of New York. I am disabled, cannot work and my only income is social security. I have a nervous condition, diabetes, blood pressure and heart trouble and a broken leg."

I could understand this letter if the debtor had gone into a county hospital in the State of New York. But she had entered a private hospital in Dade County, Florida, some two years prior to this letter. When I was working for the Welfare Department in New York City one morning the Daily News newspaper had a picture of two of our welfare recipients standing on the steps of the U.S. Embassy in Paris, France. These two ladies were asking the U.S. Consul for money to come back to New York. They had run out of funds. They had been extremely frugal in the use of their welfare checks over an extended period, bought airline tickets to France and appeared at the U.S. Embassy when their money ran out. The situations are similar.

I wouldn't want to conclude this chapter leaving you with the impression that there are no debtors who appreciate the treatment they receive from professional debt collectors.

"Gentlemen:
Attached please find my check for payment in full. I regret the inconvenience caused by this delayed payment, which resulted from my having forwarded your invoice corresponding to the total cost of surgery to the insurance company, not knowing, therefore, that you were not paid on time."

"To Royal Collection Agency:
I'm going to do all possible to pay this bill. But right now I can only make some payments until it is paid off. I'll be sending in your first payment soon."

"Here is your payment. Have a nice day."

"Dear Royal:
Enclosed please find check in the amount you requested. Thank you for being polite, patient and explicit. Please clear my name at the Credit Bureau as you said you would. You really have been wonderful. Thank you again."

"Mil pardons pour un delai concernant un paymen. C'est impossibl de l'envoyer avant." (A thousand pardons for this delayed payment. But it was impossible for me to send it before.)

One contrite patient wrote:

"Dear Doctor: Sorry for the delay in payment. My daughter thought that any mail with her name belonged to her and so I never saw any bill until some began to be received from your collection agency."

"Dear Sir: When I went to look for the receipt where I paid the bill I could not find it. I looked in the file cabinet for the portion of the bill that we keep and there I found the bill unpaid, it got put in there with the wrong group of papers. I want to apologize. It was a mistake."

Apology accepted.

Finally, when I reflect on all of the debtor letters I have read through the years I am lead to the following conclusions:

1. Only stout-hearted men and women (the kind they sing about) should make the collection profession their life-long work
2. Those people who are perfectionists and cannot settle for less from themselves or others should stay out of the collection industry
3. Those individuals who cannot stand intense criticism should not enter the debt collection industry
4. Those people who cannot find any humor in debtor letters should consider some other career

Chapter 12
Time Flies When You're Having Fun

I was a youngster when Walt Disney's Snow White and the Seven Dwarfs was first shown in the movie theaters. For me, the most memorable portion of that masterpiece was a scene in which the dwarfs sang a song. It is ingrained in my mind:

"We're busy doing nothing. Nothing the whole day long."

Here I was faced with one of my earliest dilemmas—a contradiction that I couldn't understand. How could anyone be busy doing nothing? I was raised to believe that when you were busy you were doing something and contrarily, when you were doing nothing, you were idle. And yet, here were seven dwarfs obviously enjoying themselves – they were singing and not inactive. Did it mean that when you were enjoying your work you were in reality doing nothing?

When I think of it, with the exception of my junior year in high school, a period during which I frantically searched for things to keep me busy, I have always struggled to find the time to do the things I had to do or wanted to do. When I talk to anyone who has recently retired I'm invariably told, "I don't know how I ever managed before I quit work – I stay so busy!" Is that what it means to be "busy doing nothing?

Eventually I arrived at a satisfactory solution to the dilemma. Whenever I follow closely a highly structured schedule of things to be done, I consider myself being "busy doing nothing."

For example, last Saturday morning I got out of bed when I felt like it, instead of setting the alarm. It would be nice to get out my checkbook and pay some personal bills, I thought. I took out my pen, went to my desk and sat down ready to begin this chore. I felt like having a cup of coffee first and so got up and started some hot water. I spied a few dirty dishes from last evening and thought it would be nice to surprise Johnny and rinse them, and I did just that. Before returning to my desk, I decided to go into the yard and turn on the sprinkling system since we had been short on rain last week. It was a beautiful morning, so I looked at the flowers and the grass. In the front yard I noticed an empty beer can that someone had tossed. That looked terrible, so I picked it up and put it in the garbage can. Then I noticed that one of my sprinklers was stuck and this was a good time to clean it. So I went into my garage, picked out a wrench, removed the sprinkler head and placed it into a solution of Calmal and went back into the house. For no apparent reason at that moment I remembered that the previous day an important receipt I needed slipped behind my dresser and as long as it was on my mind, what better time to retrieve it. So the day went and I never got back to writing those checks. I enjoyed the day very much and had kept myself "busy doing nothing."

The subject of time has always fascinated me. I find it interesting that we assign human qualities to it. At the end of each year we portray Father Time as an old man. The New Year we portray as a baby. We say that time "marches on." I find it equally interesting that although each of us tries to "save time," none of us has learned how to "bank" time as we do with our money. I've therefore come to the conclusion that the only advantage of saving time is to "use it" to accomplish other things that we must do or desire to do.

Long before I ever heard of the concept of "time management" I was writing lists of things to be done, and then misplacing them. That is one of my worst habits, and it causes me a great deal of grief. I very seldom lose things permanently, but every one of my "To Do" lists includes finding some things I have mislaid. I suspect the reason for this is the fact that I have too many projects going at any one time. Of course, there is a cure for this. Almost every book or article I have read on time management suggests that you must learn to say no and you must learn to delegate. The problem is that I take on more projects that I ought to by conscious design. Operating a small collection agency like mine limits the tasks that I can delegate. The team players can only do so much and the rest must be picked up by management, if done at all. So I accept the consequences and keep trying to do a better job.

Admittedly, the drain on my energy and the loss of time spent in relocating things misplaced used to be tremendous until I tried something new. Somewhere I read that when you put an object down in the absence of any other message your brain interprets the action as putting the object away. If that action was only temporary your must send a special message to the brain. So now when I am doing more than one thing at a time and temporarily lay something down I simply tell myself that the specific object must be picked up again in a matter of seconds or minutes. It works for me. Further I have assigned only one place for every object that I use and make certain that after I use it that object is returned immediately to its place. In that way it is always where it should be. It's been all of two weeks now and I haven't lost a single thing. I will wait a little longer before I claim a victory.

With more than 10,000 work days completed at RCA I doubt that there have been more than a handful of days that reached or approached what I consider to be a "perfect" work day.

8:00 A.M.-8:45 A.M. —
Arise, wash, dress, breakfast and leave for the office. (It shouldn't take any longer to accomplish all of this. Johnny says that I often look as if I really believe this. She insists that anyone who has never learned to put on a pair of socks must spend more time to dress. I keep telling her that the heel of the sock is supposed to line up with the tongue of the shoe.)

9:00 A.M.–9:30 A.M. —
Daily staff meeting. It is important to review goals at the start of each game. I want my team to know where we are now, where we were last year at this time and last month at this time. We also discuss alternative plans for making sure that we reach our goal for the day. In a small agency it's never a problem to assemble the staff. Sometimes you end up talking to yourself. Nevertheless, the discussion must go on.

10:00 A.M.–10:30 A.M. —
Go to the post office to pick up the morning mail. (Since the postmaster has informed me that they no longer have a post office box or

drawer big enough to hold all of our mail I drive to the rear platform with a pick-up truck for the bags full of payments.)

10:45 A.M.–11:45 A.M. —
Supervise opening the mail. This has to be one of the most pleasant tasks around a collection agency. All payments are identified and properly posted to each account, the deposit is prepared and the new commission figure for the day is duly noted.

11:45 A.M.–12 noon —
Deposit taken to the bank. Another record day!

12 noon–1:00 P.M. —
Lunch.

1:00 P.M.–1:30 P.M. —
Assist the supervisor who has her hands full answering the phone calls from the clients' offices reporting direct payments. We may have to put in a separate line to handle the volume of these calls!

1:30 P.M.–2:00 P.M. —
Return messages left by prospective clients inquiring about our service.

2:00 P.M.–4:00 P.M. —
Go to various clients' offices who have requested that we pick up new accounts for collection.

4:00 P.M.–4:30 P.M. —
Spend a few minutes with each member of the team to answer questions, discuss problems and solutions and commend them for their contribution to the team goals.

4:30 P.M.–5:00 P.M. —
Answer all correspondence. The letter from the President of the United States asking my advice is always on top!

Now let me tell you what actually takes place on a typical day.

5:00 A.M.–7:00 A.M. —
Quiet time, homework and planning. For a long time I have believed that each of us has a peak period of the day when we perform at our best and a low period when we accomplish very little. I am at my best in the early hours and at my worst in the late hours. So I try to take advantage of that. For the purposes of getting things done I don't think in terms of hours but rather into 15-or-30-minute blocks of time. In my morning quiet time I have either 2-30 minute blocks or 4-15 minute blocks.

Since I believe in prayer and the power of prayer, and because I'm a student of the Old and New Testaments, I can make very valuable use of my time in whatever portion I assign to my quiet period. I have also been known to play with our eight pound Pit Bull Terrier, Ginger, and to walk in our garden, looking at the flowers and trees when the sun starts to illuminate the early morning hours.

When our daughter was about four years old, she wanted a dog. Her grandparents in Louisville, Kentucky, tried to find a Boston bulldog puppy for her without success. One day a crate arrived at our house from the Railway Express Agency, and in it we found a small dirty ball that we tossed into the air. It wasn't a ball at all but an American Pit Bull terrier puppy that woke up when she hit the ground. Despite the fact that her papers listed her name as Cricket, we named her Gypsy, after the stage play Gypsy which Johnny and I had seen in New York a short time before. This was three decades before the breed was placed on the Animal Enemy #1 list for extermination. She was a member of our family for 15 years, and served as the sister our daughter never had. Alesa dressed her in clothes, put shoes on her hind paws, had make-believe tea parties with her and stomped on her tail when she didn't behave. All the time Gypsy grew to idolize her mistress and was never anything but a perfect pet.

When Gypsy died, our second pit bull, Pokey, came to live at our house, and Ginger joined the family after Pokey died. We've never had a moment's problem with any of the three and have strong feelings that the furor over the breed in general has been blown way out of proportion. In my opinion, the problem lies not with the breed but with the changes in the manner of breeding the dogs and in the behavior of the dog owners. With the rise of crime there has been a great demand for protection dogs, and breeders have hurried to meet the demand with an emphasis on developing "mean" dogs. This has led to cross breeding for "mean" traits. Likewise, owners have a responsibility to train their pets and control them properly.

I never really objected to homework when I was in school, and all through my business career I have always brought home work that I could not complete in the office. I often finish projects during my morning quiet time. That's when much of this book was written.

If I wait to plan my working day when I first come into the office in the morning, it's too late. During the planning segment of my homework time, I review the first of the three To Do lists that I maintain. The items that have been completed are removed and new ones are added as needed. Because of the nature of our business I have to be ready to adjust to the events of the work day and so this first To Do list is not necessarily arranged in the order each project will be performed.

7:00 A.M.–7:30 A.M. —
Exercise, wash and dress.

7:30 A.M.–8:45 A.M. —
Feed Ginger (if we know what's good for us), make breakfast (Johnny is one of the best cooks in the world, but breakfast is my bailiwick), wash the dishes and off to the office.

9:00 A.M.–9:30 A.M. —
My daily flight to Lucerne, Switzerland to map out my priorities for the day on my second To Do list. (On a cold and blustery September morning some years ago Johnny and I were in a hotel in Lucerne, Switzerland. Gazing out the window I saw all the local shopkeepers sweeping the sidewalks in front of their establishments. I thought that was a nice thing to do and since Royal C. A. occupied two store fronts on a busy avenue, I'm in Lucerne, Switzerland, every morning as I sweep in front of our office.)

9:30 A.M.–10:00 A.M. —
During this period I usually solve about a half dozen minor catastrophes such as "We blew a fuse," "the air conditioning isn't working," "we're out of hand towels," "the photo-stat machine is jammed," "the

computer paper order didn't arrive" or "my electric typewriter isn't working properly."

10:00 A.M.–11:00 A.M. —
Go to post office for today's mail and Pitney Bowes postage. If you're wondering why it takes an hour to go and come back from the post office, then you haven't been to one lately. Americans used to make fun of the way Europeans queue up, but we are fast becoming a nation of queuers ourselves. I usually bring some reading material to occupy my time while in line, or work on my portable To Do list that I carry around in my pocket. Usually on my way back to the office my portable telephone rings.

Either a client's office wants me to come by for some new work or my collectors want me to pick up a PIF (Payment in Full). They know where I am during the day and if they can arrange for field PIFs they are delighted and so am I. After all, that is our business, and I thoroughly enjoy meeting the debtors face to face. However, I have to be extremely careful with my time at this period of the day because between now and 2 P.M. we have a great deal of work to accomplish.

11:00 A.M.–2:00 P.M. —
Work on the mail, lunch, and prepare the deposit. Since we maintain a post office box at one post office and our street address is serviced by another post office, we still get two mail deliveries – the second coming sometime after a return from the first post office. We divide our mail into payments, correspondence, and return mail. Each is distributed to the responsible person. Matching up each payment with the proper account can be a headache, especially when a debtor sends in a payment without any identifying information, which happens several times each day. It is about this time than I am thankful I'm not posting for a utility company, for I have no doubt that their posting problems are ten times what ours are.

The posting completed, I squeeze in fifteen or twenty minutes for something to eat and then prepare the deposit. I usually arrive at the bank as the guard is locking the door. Or the guard, seeing me, knows it is time to lock the door. I could suggest that the longer I remain in business the longer it takes me to prepare the deposit, but the truth is that when I prepared my very first deposit I had to race down the five flights of stairs in the Langford Building and continue the race to the Pan American Bank two blocks away to get into the bank a second or two before the doors were locked. It has been that way ever since.

2:00 P.M.–2:30 P.M. —
A hold period. I've adapted into my schedule the same kind of hold period used by NASA. It is a good time to review my To Do lists for a forgotten item or just to take a deep breath and catch up.

2:30 P.M.–4:00 P.M. —
Field visits to client's offices and for emergencies, and/or debtors. That is, assuming there are no interruptions or emergencies, and that is a rather large assumption.

4:00 P.M.–6:00 P.M. —
Complete daily bookkeeping, computer reports and answer correspondence. There are always items that don't get finished and this is the reason for homework.

    Up to this writing I have not yet reached a point where I am convinced that I'm spending my time as wisely as possible and so I keep trying to improve. My experience has taught me that good time management is not an accident, not the result of twitching your nose or blowing into the palms of your hands. Rather, it is the end product of a conscious and concerted effort to spend your time as wisely as you spend your money. The prudent person budgets his or her money and should likewise budget his or her time. That same prudent person knows what he or she can afford to spend on any item and likewise should know how much time he or she can afford to spend on any task or project. I suspect, though, if we were to ask the public which was more important, time or money, a disproportionate group would pick money. For me, time is more important than money—if I have the time there is a good chance that I may be able to produce the money. And, despite all the statements by the experts that everyone works with the same amount of time to each 24 hours period—which is true—none of us knows when our time will run out. Again, for me the only alternative to time management is utter frustration and displeasure.

Chapter 12: Time Flies When You're Having Fun • 123

I am always preoccupied with three aspects of time: wasted time, lost time, and found time. I may allot 15 minutes for a staff meeting and before I know it an hour has passed. I stand in line at the Post Office or the bank for over forty-five minutes. A debtor may ask me to pick up a large PIF and when I get to the house the debtor is gone. All that is WASTED TIME. It disappoints me, but in each instance I was consciously engaged in a necessary task, so I accept this as the cost of doing business.

In other situations I may continuously misplace letters, reports and other various objects and I consider that LOST TIME. I become furious with myself because it is all avoidable. Whenever I am able to complete a necessary or desired task or project in a previously assigned period of time I consider this FOUND TIME and rejoice just as much as if I had found a large sum of money. The world is full of people who are constantly saying they will do this or that when they "find the time." Found time isn't discovered like a treasure; it is appropriated by conscious and persistent efforts. I am aware of the truism that says "The person who watches the clock will always be just one of the hands," but the person that doesn't watch the clock will never be able to manage his or her time properly.

Finally, while time flies when you're having fun, it is equally true that it continues to fly even when you're not having fun. The secret is to stay busy. While I thoroughly enjoy being "busy doing nothing" once in a while, I would prefer to spend the majority of my time being "busy doing something."

Chapter 13
Collections from Cave Man to the Computer

My intent here is neither to discuss the relative merits of the biblical and scientific theories of creation, nor to rewrite history. Thanks to the archeologists, historians and sociologists throughout the centuries, we are able to trace the origin of man (Ed. note: Had Gerry written this book today he would have used inclusive terminology. BBG) back to the Paleolithic Period which lasted for perhaps one million years, and ended sometime around 8000 B.C.

I have no difficulty visualizing some distant ancestor of mine living in a cave and, being accosted for the very first time by some large animal, instinctively reaching for the nearest object to protect himself. It may have been a heavy branch of a tree or even a rock, but when it accomplished its purpose, he really took a huge step forward for mankind. He had invented a tool and soon he probably recognized the fact that if he tied a rock to a portion of that branch, he could get more leverage. And then he probably reasoned that if he could chip off a portion of that rock it would be much lighter. And so he had an effective axe for hunting food and chopping wood for his fire, for protection, and to enable him to make his cave more livable.

The cave men and women continued to collect more tools. The tools were more advanced as their curiosity lead them into adventures, as their development took place over those one million years, and as they searched for food for their families. As it is to this day, not everyone has the same abilities and I'm sure there were some cave men that enjoyed making tools, and others who were happy hunting animals, and still others who enjoyed neither tool making nor hunting but preferred to draw pictures on the walls of the caves.

Eventually, some enterprising cave man made a deal with his neighbor in an adjoining cave. "I'll trade you some of my tools for some of the animals you've killed." The deal was struck. The hunter added, "By the way, my axe broke yesterday, so if you let me have one of your axes I promise to bring you back three freshly dressed wild pigs when I return from the hunt tomorrow." That sounded real good to the tool maker, so he gave the axe to the hunter and went back to his cave, crawled up on a rock and dreamed of his dinner tomorrow night. That was the very first extension of credit. But when the following night came and the hunter hadn't returned he went to the hunter's cave and found it empty. And so was born the first collection problem.

The tool maker was outraged. He wanted his due, so off he went with all the weapons he possessed, and with whatever manpower he could muster, and if he was stronger than the hunter and could locate him, he took not only his three pigs but everything belonging to the hunter, including his entire family, and probably left the hunter dead. Such has always been the case and always will be on the frontier. Incidentally, that was also the very first PIF.

The experts tell us they know the world's oldest profession and I will not quarrel with them. But I do know the second and third oldest professions. The second oldest is credit, perhaps as early as ninety days after the first. The third oldest profession is collections, perhaps as early as ninety days after the second.

In his *An Encyclopedia of World History* (Houghton Mifflin), William Langer describes how the prehistoric period ended with a dramatic change in the climate. "The disappearance of the last ice-sheet which marked the end of the Pleistocene period, led to the rise of a new culture…The big animals of the Pleistocene on which the Paleolithic hunters had largely depended for their food disappeared everywhere except in parts of Africa, and their place was taken by the present-day fauna. Also with the ice retreat new regions were opened to settlement…The next stage of development, the Neolithic, is marked by the invention and almost universal adoption of four important new features: agriculture, domesticated animals, pottery and polished (instead of chipped) stone tools. These changes and the results which followed from them were revolutionary. Man ceased being a nomad, eternally following his food supply and became a sedentary being, residing and growing his food in one spot. He now had an assured food supply to carry over lean seasons and this led to a great increase in the population…The altered conditions likewise made possible the accumulation of possessions, the creation and satisfaction of new needs, the leisure for invention and speculation, the growth of large communities and cities, the development of more complex social organization, and in fact all progress that has taken place since that time."

It is therefore not surprising to read elsewhere that the patriarch Isaac amassed a great fortune.

"That year Isaac's crops were tremendous – 100 times the grain he sowed…He was soon a man of great wealth and became richer and richer. He had large flocks of sheep and goats, great herds of cattle and many servants." (Genesis 26:12-14)

His son, Jacob, likewise became successful as his flocks "increased rapidly and he became very wealthy, with many servants, camels, and donkeys." (Genesis 30:43)

Jacob's son, Joseph, at about 30 years of age probably became one of the first professional bill collectors when he entered the service of the king of Egypt as business administrator of the entire country. There is no doubt in my mind that, with the backing of the pharaoh, Joseph was a very effective collector, among his other chores.

It seems plausible to me that soon after the first man and woman walked this earth they also learned the necessity of adhering to certain self-imposed rules for survival, such as never turn your back on a dinosaur, never allow the fire at the entrance to your cave burn out, never wander too far from your cave at night, and never leave your cave without an axe. As time went on, I'm sure the list of rules grew, and it became necessary for someone to be responsible for passing on the rules to the newest members of each family. Probably, the oldest survivor accepted this duty.

As the population increased and families began to live in community with other families, those who were chosen to lead not only picked individuals to carry on the duty, but also added some rules of their own. Eventually these rules were written down. What is perhaps one of the most ancient written rules, if not the oldest one concerning man's commerce, is also the very foundation upon which the collection profession is built. It is founded in the Decalogue (The Ten Commandments) and is commonly known as the eighth commandment: "You must not steal." (Exodus 20:15)

From the very beginning of mankind, everyone has been expected to pay for goods and services they receive. Basic to all written law in civilized societies is not only the rights that persons enjoy but their responsibilities as well. The fact that there are so many references to indebtedness in the Old and New Testaments of the Bible suggests to me that collection activity was prevalent through the fourth century A.D. in Palestine and everywhere else in the civilized world of that day.

While there were no bankruptcy laws at that time, we read:

"Every fiftieth year on the Day of Atonement let the trumpets blow loud and long throughout the land. For the fiftieth year shall behold, a time to proclaim liberty throughout the land to all enslaved debtors, and a time for the cancelling of all public and private debts." (Leviticus 25:10)

It was called the Year of Jubilee from the Hebrew word "jobcl," meaning "ram's horn," which was blown to call attention to this celebration. It was the custom of that time for debtors to declare themselves destitute and sell themselves to wealthy or influential individuals to pay for their debts. If the buyer happened to be an Israelite, the debtor could not be treated as a slave but as a servant until the Year of the Jubilee at which time he could return to his family and possessions. If, on the other hand, the buyer was a foreigner, the Israelite debtor could be redeemed at any time by paying his benefactor.

"The price of his freedom shall be in proportion to the number of years left before the Year of Jubilee – whatever it would cost to hire a servant for that number of years. If there are still many years until the Jubilee, he shall pay almost the amount he received when he sold himself; if the years have passed and only a few remain until the Jubilee, then he will repay only a small portion of the amount he received when he sold himself…If he has not been redeemed by the time of the year of the Jubilee arrives, then he and his children shall be freed at that time." (Leviticus 25:50-54)

Two thoughts enter my mind. First, it just makes good sense that smart debtors would try to declare themselves destitute as close to

Jubilee as possible and then try to get the highest price possible. Second, since the average age of individuals was not very high at that time it appears that a person unlucky enough to sell himself just after the Jubilee probably never made it until the next one.

We get another glimpse of debt collecting around the second century A.D. as we read:

"Come to terms quickly with your enemy (creditor) before it is too late and he drags you into court and you are thrown into a debtor's cell, for you will stay there until you have paid the last penny." (Matthew 5:25-26)

The Abingdon Bible Commentary describes the quote by Jesus from his Sermon on the Mount, "The importance of paying one's debts at the right time is stressed to secure the welfare of society." (Abingdon Press)

When Christ was asked whether he believed it was right to pay taxes to the Roman government, he asked for a coin and further asked the Pharisees to identify the face stamped on it. When they answered that it was Caesar, he replied, "Render therefore to Caesar the things that are Caesar's, and to God the things that are God's." (Matthew 22:21) It is my opinion that Christ's meaning was in the broadest sense, going beyond just paying the Roman tax. Once again, I think he was emphasizing the importance of paying one's bills.

Matthew writes of a debtor who owed a king a sum of money that today would amount to $10 million. Since the man couldn't pay this, the king ordered him sold for the debt, along with his wife, children and everything they owned. The debtor fell down on his knees and begged for more time, assuring the king that he would eventually pay the entire bill in full. The king not only released him but forgave the entire debt. (Such magnanimity!) That was not the end of the story, though. The very same man left the king and went to someone who owed him $2,000. He grabbed his debtor by the throat and demanded payment in full immediately. He, too, pleaded for more time and also promised payment in full in due time. The debtor who had been forgiven the larger debt would not forgive the debtor with the smaller debt and had him thrown into jail until the bill was paid in full. (Matthew 18:23-30)

Finally, in the Lord's Prayer, Matthew uses this form: "And forgive us our debts, as we also have forgiven our debtors." (Matthew 6:12)

Considering the fact that Luke had written about this same prayer of Jesus, only earlier, and that he had used the word "sins" instead of "debts," I find Matthew's choice of words significant. In view of the many scenes of debtors in his gospel and the admonitions to pay one's bills, I cannot help entertaining the thought that quite possibly Matthew could have been moonlighting as a bill collector when he was collecting taxes before he joined Jesus Christ as an apostle. What do we know about him? According to Edgar Goodspeed in his book, *The Twelve: the Story of Christ's Apostles*, being a tax collector he probably knew the Greek language. His toll office may have been on the Mediterranean-Damascus Road. Certainly he knew how to read and write and he had to keep accurate records of the names, amounts paid and the originating addresses and final destinations of the travelers. (Winston Co.) No doubt he was approached by many businessmen for his help in either collecting their bills or in providing addresses where they could locate their debtors. For these very same reasons I suspect Zacchaeus, one of the most influential Jews in the Roman Tax collecting business, may also have been collecting delinquent bills.

From the ancient Brehon Laws of Ireland we get this interesting glimpse of debtor-creditor relations. These laws began around the first century A.D. and continued through 1169 A.D. when the first English invaders came to that island.

In *The Story of the Irish Race*, Seumas MacManus describes part of the Brehon Law. "A fasc (summons) was first served upon the debtor, after which, if the debt was not paid, a gabail (distress) was laid upon some portion of his property – almost always on his livestock...There was an "anan" (stay) of a day or days to give the debtor a second chance of paying. If he did not pay within the "anan," the distrained goods were lifted — the cattle, say driven off, and placed in a pound. An "apad" (notice) was then served upon the debtor, telling him that the cattle were taken, and informing him just where they were impounded. Then followed a "dithin," another stay, to give the debtor yet another chance for redeeming his property. If, when the "dithin" had expired, the debtor had not redeemed his property, the next stage, the "lobad" (wasting) began: that is, instead of selling all of the seized property for the immediate and complete satisfying of the debt, it was sold in portions — out of still further regard for, and mercy toward the debtor. But if...the debtor denied the claim and demanded trial of the case – or if he agreed to pay after the expiration of a certain time – he got a stay of execution on giving pledge (gell), or giving bail. If then, the debtor did not fulfill the conditions of the stay of execution, the pledge, or the bail was forfeited and the levying of the distress proceeded. Sometimes he gave his own son in pledge… In that case the services of the son were forfeit, if the conditions were not fulfilled, the son became bondsman of the creditor until the debt was worked out. If he had been bailed the "arhire" (bailsman) became the creditor's bondsman, in the same case, if he could not meet the liabilities of him who he had bailed." (Devin-Adair Co.)

Things apparently became a bit more complicated in those days if the debtor was of superior rank to the creditor. When that occurred, the creditor had to first try "fasting" upon his debtor before he could proceed with legal action. MacManus further describes this practice.

"The creditor sat himself down by the door of the dishonest or unjust one and while the sympathetic world looked on, and its indignation daily grew greater against the wronger who had forced the wronged to take this extreme course, the latter tasted no food. In short it was a plain hunger strike for compelling justice from the powerful."

If this debtor of higher rank felt that he was innocent of the debt he had the right to "fast" upon the creditor. In that case it was assumed that the one who was capable of fasting the longest was telling the truth.

Recently, the Queen of England announced her "Honors List" – the names of her subjects who have made significant achievements. I imagine that 20 centuries ago the subjects of the monarchies traveled to "Fairs" to learn of such honors; also to participate in important affairs of state with the royal family.

"At the fair, going to it and returning from it, no oppressed debtor could be molested, arrested, or distrained for his debt. On the eve of a "feis" or fair, all personal ornaments, rings, bracelets, or broaches, that had been pawned to relieve financial distress, or impounded for debts overdue, must, for the time of the assemblage be released to their owners. The creditor who refused to release them was heavily fined for the mental suffering caused to those who were forced to the disgrace of appearing without adornment at the great festive gatherings, whereat all the nation appeared in its richest, most beautiful and best."

For those who argue that it is only in recent days that women receive anywhere near the treatment they deserve, it is enlightening to learn that even in the 5th century Ireland, "a married woman retained the right, too, in her own person to pursue a case at law, and in her own person to recover for debt. In this connection if may be mentioned that when a woman levied upon the goods of a debtor, she distrained such things as were appropriate for women; such animals, for instance as lap-dogs or sheep; such articles as spindles, mirrors, or comb bags."

There is one particular collection by the high king of Tara in first century Ireland that deserves mention at this point. It has come to be known as the "Boru Tribute" (Cow Tribute) and its affect was felt for a period of at least 500 years. The High King Tuathal had two daughters, one of whom he gave in marriage to King Eochaid of the province of Leinster. Eochaid apparently tired of his wife, or lusted for her sister. He let it be known that she had died and sought sympathy from his father-in-law. (In fact, he had imprisoned his wife in a tower.) King Tuathal in time gave his second daughter in marriage to Eochaid. We can imagine the grief at this deception when the two sisters came upon each other sometime later. It is said the grief stricken sisters died, and when their father learned what had happened, he gathered the full power of his position and marched into Leinster prepared to destroy his son-in-law's and the entire province. The only thing saving them all was Eochaid's "binding the province to pay… every alternative year for an indefinite period…five thousand cows, five thousand hogs, five thousand cloaks, five thousand vessels of brass and bronze and five thousand ounces of silver."

From about the middle of the 13th century until the Debtors Act of 1869 English Law allowed imprisonment of debtors. In the American colonies before the Revolutionary War people were also imprisoned for debt. From as early as 1776, provisions in law prohibited such action. Eventually, by 1836, with some slight exceptions, imprisonment for debt was abolished in the United States.

Forty years later an event was to take place that certainly revolutionized the collection industry. Alexander Graham Bell invented the telephone in 1876. To be sure, people didn't rush out to open collection agencies. Since telephones were considered a luxury and not a necessity, the majority of people didn't own one. In time, the telephone became a necessity and today almost everyone has at least one, or can be reached at home, at his or her place of employment, or through friends or relatives.

Just 6 years before the telephone, the first typewriter was introduced for commercial use. V.L. Campbell recounts the impact of this invention in his book, *The Saga of the American Collectors Association*. (Jones Press) "In the early part of the twentieth century...W. A. Shryer, Detroit, Michigan, was selling a complete mail order course of instruction in collection work under the title of the American Collection Service. He was also editor and publisher of an efficient little collection magazine called Business Service. Mr. Shryer's home study material and the magazine...were in no small way responsible for the fact that collection agencies were springing up in all parts of the country."

State associations of collectors were also springing up with the west coast leading the way. The California association was encouraging collectors to organize in every state, and their trade publication, The Collector, was made available to collectors throughout the country and served... "to pinpoint the rights and obligations of collectors and to encourage their attendance and participation at conventions in addition to their organization and self-regulation."

On June 22, 1939, at a joint meeting of the California Association (then celebrating its 22nd anniversary) and the Pacific Coast Association of Collectors (then celebrating its 15th anniversary), the American Collectors Association was formed. It has grown into the largest association of professional debt collectors in the world with more than 3,400 national and international member agencies.

In the annals of the U.S. professional debt collectors, the 1970's will be remembered as the "decade of legislation." Prompted by the expose' of isolated collector abuses around the country, and most dramatically in Chicago, our industry braced itself against public outcry for laws to protect debtors from agency harassment. The result was a proliferation of state collection agency licensing laws, capped by the Federal Fair Debt Collection Practices Act, which serves us as our "Bible" of Do's and Don'ts.

We are an industry of great change and new technology. The introduction of computerized offices and computerized billing services has revolutionized the industry once more. But the story doesn't end there.

As our industry is poised to celebrate its Golden Anniversary in 1989, computerized telephone dialing systems are already enabling us to increase our attempted phone contacts daily from 90-100 to up to 700.

It may seem trite to say that we have come a long way from the cave man days. Even a cursory review of the history of man since he first appeared on this planet leaves me with a sense of awe at his ability to adapt in every age. In the area of business, man has always been able to meet his needs by inventing and manufacturing, marketing, and then making provisions for collecting the slow paying and delinquent accounts. What proportions this will assume in the future fills me with a sense of great expectations.

Chapter 14
I Had the Craziest Dream

This was going to be one of those days for which Miami is famous, and one the likes of which very few other cities in the world can boast. My clock-radio woke me during the weather portion of the 4:30 A.M. capsule news. Clear and sunny skies were predicted, with a high of 78 degrees and a low of 65, seas smooth to a light chop, winds of 5 to 10 miles per hour, and the pollution factor in the good range. Considering that this was the middle of February and the Midwest was in the grip of a furious snowstorm, the plains states were shivering because of wind chill factors in the minus 60's, and the east coast from Atlanta to Maine was resting under a blanket of 2 to 3 inches of newly fallen snow, we were very fortunate.

I had a particular reason why I wanted to get to the office earlier than usual this morning. There was a distinct possibility that on this day the Royal Collection Agency would be the first collection agency in the United States to be struck by an employee union. My mind quickly reviewed all of the events in the past three weeks leading up to this moment.

One of my telephone collectors had been selected as the spokesperson for the entire staff. She came to me with a list of grievances.

1. We demand a starting wage for every employee of $675 per week.

2. It is cruel and unusual punishment for telephone collectors to be required to call debtors for more than eight continuous hours. We demand that the work week consist of eight hours on and eight hours off, and demand further that RCA hire an alternate staff to cover each employee's off time.

3. We demand that no telephone collector be required to call on any account under $300.

4. We demand that no telephone collector be required to work on any account where incomplete information has been furnished by the client. Complete information is the debtor's phone numbers at home and work.

5. We demand that RCA, every thirty days, must take out a full page ad in the Miami Herald and the Miami Daily News, urging the debtor public to refrain from harassing telephone collectors, reminding debtors that collectors are people, too.

Accompanying this list of demands was a lengthy report from a prestigious national research organization. It concluded that professional telephone collectors are subjected to more pressure and tension than air traffic controllers. Funny, I mused to myself. And I always thought I was a fairly good employer, sensitive to the needs of my employees. Now they have gone too far. When I rejected the demands as impossible, they went to the Teamsters Union, which agreed to admit them into the Professional Telephone Collectors of America, and promised to make Royal Collection Agency a test case in their effort to organize the entire industry.

The harder I tried to hurry to the office, the slower my mind, my legs, and my arms worked. It seemed as if I were functioning at half-speed. I probably could have moved faster if I were under water. As I approached the main intersection of N.E. 6th Ave. and N.E. 125th St. in North Miami (our office is in the 12300 block) I noticed that a policeman had blocked off the entire street and was directing all traffic east to N.E. 6th Court. I could not see any vehicles from 125th St. south to 123rd St., only crowds of people. Had there been an auto accident? I would soon find out.

I snaked up and down several blocks, trying to get closer to the office, but to no avail. I counted 387 men, women and children, all obstructing traffic in the area of our office. There was even one of these mobile sandwich and coffee vans catering to the crowd. Under the circumstances, I would have liked to turn north at 6th Ave. and drive around the block to see where the line was headed but, again, the police had cordoned off the block, and traffic was detoured westward.

I ducked into our parking lot in the rear of the office, and knocked on our back door, hoping that the employees had shown up. They were there, all right, but greeted me coldly. Their spokesperson informed me that they had called off the strike temporarily and had decided to work, but to practice "guerilla warfare" on the job. I shouted, "That's not only unfair, but it's illegal!"

"No, it's not," they replied in unison as they handed me a six foot long affidavit, affirming in large print that the employees had every right to sabotage the business. It was signed by the governor of Florida and the mayors of North Miami and Dade County, Florida.

I was heading for my desk when I heard someone say, "You have another problem, boss. There's a crowd of people waiting outside to pay their bills. What'll we do?"

"Take their money," I offered. Why in the world did they have to wait for me to say that? We quickly set up a long portable table in the waiting room and I assigned three of my employees to process the payments. The policeman stationed at the front door let in a dozen people at a time. Snails moved faster than my workers today. I knew they were all at their telephones, calling debtors, because I could see their lips moving, but no sounds were coming out. Only continuous collection forms in multicolor emanated from their mouths, eventually covering the entire office floor.

Luckily, I received two telephone calls that required me to leave the office. I was glad for the opportunity to get out, because I couldn't stop worrying about all the ways my employees could sabotage my business before the day was over, and because I was certain that by day's end the entire office would be inundated with those collection form letters.

The first call was from the treasurer of one of my clients. It was a medical office that consisted of 25 doctors that worked out of as many hospitals in the Dade and Broward County area. He had to see me immediately, but would not discuss the reason. I said I'd be there. The second call came from the chairman of the board of an 800-bed hospital. During the past year we had several meetings to discuss the possibility of our handling all their collection problems. They had come to a decision and he wanted to see me without fail today. He wouldn't reveal their decision over the phone. Again I agreed.

Arriving at my first appointment, the treasurer ushered me into his office and locked the door. "How long have you represented us?" he asked.

"38 years," I replied.

"That's right. And we are still very happy with your collection recovery. What are we paying you now?"

"50% on a contingent basis – no collection, no charge," I answered.

"Exactly," he countered. "From now on the rate must be 15%."

That took the wind right out of me. "You must be kidding," I objected. "We cannot make a living at that rate. Why, the first class rate of postage is now $1.25 and will go up to $1.50 next month." He sat calmly as I presented all my arguments for maintaining the current rate. He simply said, "We are not interested at all whether or not you make a living."

"I CANNOT AGREE TO THAT RATE CHANGE!" I shouted. Apparently, he could not hear me because he just smiled and said he was glad that I saw it their way. He handed me a pen to sign a paper confirming our new agreement. I threw the pen down, but it strangely floated down on the agreement and signed my name for me. I found myself smiling back and shaking his hand and telling him how much we enjoyed working for his group.

It was no time at all before I was seated in the board room of the hospital that I was hoping to represent. The chairman of the board introduced me to the people seated at the table – two comptrollers, two collection managers, two supervisors, two collectors, two patients, two doctors, two nurses, two orderlies, two technicians, two cooks, two maintenance men, and two security guards. There was a knock on the door, and two bookkeepers entered and sat at the remaining two chairs. I was told that a year-long search for a collection agency to represent them had been concluded, and Royal had been chosen. All I had to do was sign the contract, which was now being brought into the room on a huge silver platter by two waitresses. There was no need to read it, I was told, just simply sign it and get right to work collecting their bills.

"If you don't mind, I would like to glance at the agreement," I said, the businessman in me taking over.

"All right," the chairman replied. "But make it fast. We don't have all day."

There were 127 pages to the agreement, and it took me over one hour just to speed read it. "Is it agreed?" the chairman asked.

"I'd like to ask some questions," I replied.

"That's a bit out of the ordinary," they all shouted in unison, "but go ahead and ask your questions."

First, I asked them why they felt the need to require RCA to provide a $10 billion surety bond to protect the hospital. Wasn't that a bit excessive?

Second, I wondered why they had left our percentage fee blank. While they felt that matter could be negotiated, I felt we should settle that matter in the beginning. They must have had a direct pipeline connection to my previous appointment because I was told that their current collection agency was receiving 10%, but that they would agree to pay us 15%.

Third, I asked them how often we would receive new accounts for collection. Their answer was, "Whenever we feel like it."

"How do you report direct payments made to you?" I wondered. They told me that would not present any problem. Any time a debtor insisted that he or she had sent money to them, all I had to do was have the debtor present to me a photocopy of both sides of the cancelled checks and only then could I get credit for collecting the bill. "What if the debtor refuses to comply with that requirement or is unable to do so?" I asked. "Well, in that case, we keep the payment and you don't get credit." Again they replied in unison, with that horrible chuckle.

I had noticed that the contract required a monthly check from RCA to them for gross collections, along with our statement. "How long would I have to wait for my commission check?" There was a long silence while one of the bookkeepers left the room to search for my answer. Twenty minutes later she returned and whispered her discovery into the chairman's ear. "We can guarantee that you'll receive your check within 6 months." Again a chuckle rippled throughout the room. I explained to the entire group that we were a collection agency, not a bank, and they politely nodded their heads and smiled at me.

"NO MORE QUESTIONS!" announced the chairman. "Sign the contract now." I vaguely remember saying something to the effect that while I appreciated the opportunity to represent the hospital, under the circumstances I would have to decline. I started to get up to leave, but seemed to be glued in the seat of the chair, and I also couldn't lift my hands from the arms of the chair. Now they laughed out loud as the chairman signed my name to the contract, they all signed as witnesses, and wished me well in my new assignment. Magically, I was released from my chair, able to get up and leave. I was so relieved that I shook hands with everyone in the room and thanked them for selecting us.

On my way back to my office I called my office manager on my car phone. She told me that the line of debtors with payments still stretched around the block, and that the payments were being processed very slowly. They had been so busy that no one had picked up the mail at the Post Office, and she asked me to do that. I asked her to call our bank to ask them to stay open as long as necessary for us to make a deposit.

I reached the Post Office and picked up the largest bundle of mail I had ever seen. There was something else strange about it. Usually we get a bag full of our printed return envelopes with payments in them, along with a few pieces of returned mail. Today, however, there was no returned mail and no small payment envelopes; only large manila envelopes with identical printed labels to Royal Collection Agency, but each one was from a different debtor. There were 136 of them.

Around 4:30 P.M. I was finally seated at my desk, ready to open mail. The crowd of debtors continued to mill about in the outer office, along with several police officers. They were struggling through the ocean of paper, now swirling around chest level, which continued to emanate from the mouths of my telephone collectors. In a way, I was relieved that they were leaving at 5 P.M., although I could have used their help late into the night, since there were still at least 100 debtors waiting to pay their bills. But none of my employees would volunteer to stay even one minute past quitting time. Now I understood what they had meant by "practicing guerilla warfare" on the job.

My office manager was the last employee to leave the office. She told me that the bank had agreed to keep one teller on until I arrived with the deposit. I processed the remaining debtors' payments myself until 9:00 P.M., and when the last one left I thanked the police for their help and locked the door. I still had the mail to open and the deposit to prepare.

I was both disappointed and a bit relieved when I realized that there wasn't a single payment in the entire mail. Every large envelope contained the same mimeographed message:

DEAR ROYAL:
CONCERNING MY BILL PLEASE BE ADVISED THAT I WILL PAY YOU AS MUCH AS I CAN AS OFTEN AS I CAN. THERE IS NO NEED TO CONTACT ME AGAIN. IN FACT, IF I EVER HEAR FROM YOU AGAIN I WILL NEVER PAY A PENNY.

Each letter was signed by a different debtor. It was the first time in my life that I was happy about having no money in the mail, since I already had well over 400 payments to list on the bank deposit slips.

At 11:45 P.M. I left the office for the bank, made the deposit, thanked the teller for waiting for me, and headed home. I collapsed into bed as the late late movie was beginning on television.

It seemed only minutes before my clock radio awakened me with the weather portion of the 4:30 A.M. capsule news. They were expecting rainy cold weather with a high of 60 and a low of 48, choppy seas, winds up to 20 miles per hour, and the pollution factor was missing. I told you I had the craziest dream!

"I mailed you a payment last night."

Chapter 15
Having the Last Word

Before I proceed any farther I must admit here that I have always had the greatest admiration for anyone who has ever taken pen to paper, brush to canvas, fingers to clay, hammer to nail or cement to bricks and allowed their imagination to soar.

Now that I am approaching the final period of the last sentence of this book I feel not unlike a pregnant woman who has just delivered. I thoroughly enjoyed conceiving the idea and as it grew in my mind and took shape on paper I was even a bit proud of that accomplishment. Still later, there were moments of pleasure and displeasure as I contemplated the success or failure of this venture. Lately, I have been anxious for the "birth" to take place. And now that it is here I suppose I join the ranks of my predecessors in hoping that my creation will be treated kindly.

As I allow my mind to wander back over the events of the past three decades to the very first time I dialed a debtor and asked for payment in full, I am amazed how well the collection industry has treated me. I have had my share of failures, but I have always tried to remain humble in the face of success and resolute in the face of reverses. I am thankful constantly for the opportunities, challenges, and experiences that have been mine. Those who are part of the general public, whose only contact with bill collectors had been through an occasional television script or newspaper expose, may very well rate us with undertakers, medical examiners and dog catchers. I am not naïve enough to believe that I have persuaded you to enter our industry. Hopefully though, something said in the previous pages has convinced you of the necessity of our work.

I exhort my colleagues and fellow bill collectors to take pride in their work. Always strive to do your very best even if you cannot be the best. (As I write this the XV Winter Olympics have drawn to a close and many people are disappointed that we Americans came home with so few medals. Typically American, we've appointed a commission to determine why we did so poorly and to devise a plan for doing better the next time. In my eyes, everyone who participated and gave their very best effort was a winner, too.) Remember, we are part of a long line of specialists that goes back to the very beginning of commerce itself.

I am pleased to inform you who are the clients of collection agencies around the world that while during the past three decades almost everything in our industry has been subject to change, there are two notable exceptions: our purpose and our responsibility, which I defined for my personal benefit in the beginning. It was to "offer the finest complete collection service that experience and ability can provide" and "at all times to represent the complete interests of our clients within the framework of established business practices, the law and common sense." I believe they are still worthy and valid goals.

Finally, if you are currently receiving letters and phone calls from collection agencies, I urge you to avoid the temptation to become what I call an "if only" person. "If only" people tend to react to the problem by rationalizing, "If only I hadn't taken ill, (…I had a better paying job…I had more money in the bank) I wouldn't be in this predicament." They spend so much time bemoaning their problem that they end up doing little to solve it. "In spite of" people will rise above the immediate problem: "in spite of the illness," (…not having a better job…not having more money in the bank). The result is usually action that eliminates the problem immediately or brings them closer to the solution.

I assure you that you will always find the truly professional debt collector anxious to help you out of your dilemma. The truly professional debt collector will never embarrass you or harass you or talk down to you. For the truly professional debt collector knows only too well that in a sense we are all debtors and that it behooves every one of us to remember to add to our daily thoughts and prayers these words, "AND FORGIVE US OUR DEBTS…"

About the Authors

Gerry

Born is Queens, New York, Gerry Gould was a studious young man, devouring as many self-help and positive thinking books as he could. It was this early introduction to positive thinking that inspired Gerry to become a leading proponent of taking the bull by the horns and riding it. Gerry was always a person who followed his heart and stepped out on faith.

Gerry attended the undergraduate and graduate schools of New York University. While in graduate school, he visited his beloved maternal grandmother, Adele, and her husband who had a debt collection agency in Miami, Florida. Gerry returned to Queens and told his professor and advisor that he was moving to Miami, much to their chagrin. His grandmother sold the Royal Collection Agency to Gerry soon afterward. Determined to succeed, Gerry went feet-first into business with his sink-or-swim attitude.

For four decades Gerry was a professional debt collector. As a certified instructor for the American Collectors Association (ACA) Gerry became a teacher and mentor to collection agents all over the United States. And he served on the committee to draft the Fair Debt Collection Laws, many of which are still in effect.

Gerry was preceded in death by his first wife, Johnalene Marie (Johnny). They had one married daughter, Alesa Gambrell (John) of Greenville, South Carolina. Gerry's hobbies were reading, traveling and gardening.

After Johnny's death Gerry met B.B. in their Methodist Church. Discovering they had many similar experiences and interests, they dated, fell in love and married all in one year. Unfortunately, while preparing for their one year anniversary trip Gerry suffered a fatal heart attack.

Debra

Debra Ciskey is the Director of Compliance in the Receivables Management division at Afni, Inc., in Bloomington, Illinois. Debra joined Afni, Inc., in September, 1993. During her tenure at Afni, Debra created and drove training and development programs and created and manages Afni's compliance management system in Afni's Receivables Management organization.

Prior to joining Afni, Debra was on the staff of the American Collectors Association, Inc, now known as ACA International, where she was the assistant director of Public Affairs for 5 years and subsequently served as Director of Education for 8 years. In her public affairs role, Debra helped to develop the association's compliance program for members, monitored state and federal legislation related to the debt collection industry, planned the association's annual Legislative Conference, and wrote a number of monthly newsletters. As Director of Education, she was responsible for leading the team that developed and implemented the association's education program for members all over the U.S. She was also responsible for programming for the association's annual international convention and expo. In addition, Debra trained and managed the Education Department's faculty, a group of more than 50 ACA members who underwent a rigorous selection and training process.

Debra is actively involved in ACA International (ACA). Since joining Afni, Debra has served as a member of ACA's Public Relations committee, SRO Task Force, Education Council, Online Committee, Ethics Committee and Asset Buyers Division Committee. Debra regularly presents at ACA's annual international convention and expo as well as other ACA conferences. She is currently a member of the association's Board of Directors. Debra is also active in the Illinois Collectors Association (ICA) on behalf of Afni, having served as president in 2009-2010.

In 1998, Debra received the ACA Enterprises Award of Merit for her contributions during her term as chairman of ACA's Online Committee, specifically for work performed on the development of ACA's initial website for ACA members. In 2000, Debra was inducted into ACA's International Fellowship of Certified Collection Executives. In 2004, she was awarded the Fred Kirschner Instructor Achievement Award for having taught more than 50 seminars in her career as an ACA instructor, earned the award repeatedly as she surpassed milestones in her active teaching career. To date, she has taught nearly 180 ACA seminars. Ciskey was named the association's Instructor of the Year in 2005.

In 2007, Debra was named one of the Top 50 Most Influential Collection Professionals by Collection Advisor Magazine. She is the current compliance columnist for the magazine.

Debra holds an MA in Organizational Management from the University of Phoenix and a BA in English and Secondary Education from Iowa State University. Debra is also a Professional Collection Specialist (ACA) and holds ACA's Scholar and Fellow Degrees in Collection Business Management. In 2009, Debra earned ACA International's Credit and Collection Compliance Officer Diploma. Debra lives in Normal, Illinois, is married to Mark Ciskey, with whom she raised two children, Dan and Amelia. She is the bulletin editor for Epiphany Parish, where she also serves as Sacristan. In addition to her work on *And Forgive Us Our Debts*, Debra has edited three murder mysteries, a book of poetry, and a family history book for a fellow parishioner and author.

B.B.

Born in Cincinnati, Ohio, B.B. grew up in Miami, Florida. After graduating from the University of South Florida, she taught biology in the Miami Public School System. Five years later she earned her graduate degree from Emory University to become a school library media specialist. During her thirtieth year with the school system, another path opened up for her: she pursued a lifelong interest in massage therapy. Retiring from education in 2001 she achieved her goal to become a licensed massage therapist. In addition to her practice B.B. has returned to her first love of teaching and offers classes for massage students.

Her first book, *GG's Principle: Three Steps to Empower You in Any Situation*, was published in 2011. It was inspired by Gerry's ninety eight words he lived by. As a healer, author and educator, B.B. is available for motivational speaking.

B.B. is a member of the Florida State Massage Therapy Association, Daughters of the American Revolution, Natives of Dade, South Florida Palm Society and Fulford United Methodist Church. Known as the "punster" her hobbies include singing, gardening, swimming, golfing and public speaking. B.B. shares a tropical home with her two Boston Terriers, Grace and Joy.

Notes

Made in the USA
Charleston, SC
07 June 2014